DOCUMENTS OF MODERN HISTORY

General Editors:

A. G. Dickens

The Director, Institute of Historical Research, University of London

Alun Davies

Professor of Modern History, University College, Swansea

72811

THE LIBRARY
ST. MARY'S COLLEGE OF MARYLAND
ST. MARY'S CITY, MARYLAND 20686

THE GROWTH OF
THE BRITISH
COMMONWEALTH
1880-1932

edited by

I. M. Cumpston

Reader in Commonwealth History,
Birkbeck College, University of London

St. Martin's Press   New York

© I. M. Cumpston 1973

All rights reserved. For information, write:
St. Martin's Press, Inc., 175 Fifth Avenue, New York, N.Y. 10010

Printed in Great Britain

Library of Congress Catalog Card Number: 72–94816
First published in the United States of America in 1973

AFFILIATED PUBLISHERS:
Macmillan and Company, Limited, London—also at Bombay,
Calcutta, Madras and Melbourne—The Macmillan Company of
Canada, Limited, Toronto

CONTENTS

PREFACE

When this series was inaugurated, it was agreed that there should not be a separate section on Ireland as there is a volume on Ireland projected in the series. There is also no separate section on India. In view of the scale of the book—less than 200 pages—which conforms with the series, a great many extracts have been taken from documents published by the British Government or prepared for official purposes. Special use has been made of memoranda drawn up for the British Cabinet and printed British parliamentary papers. I have also taken extracts from Hansard's parliamentary debates. The scale of the book has virtually precluded the use of official documents from the Dominions or dependent territories. Rather have I sought to give coherence to the theme by concentrating on the evolution of British policy. While this is open to the criticism that it over-emphasises the British aspect, this may be countered by the argument that until 1932 it was still the *British* Commonwealth and Empire, that the British Crown remained its head, and the British Cabinet continued to bear responsibility for Imperial matters, subject to the extent to which the Dominions had sought and won responsibility for matters involving their interests.

It may be argued that the documents chosen do not adequately represent the views of unofficial bodies outside the British Government. Memoranda prepared for the British Cabinet were, however, drafted in many offices and drew extensively on official files; they frequently embodied reports and views from unofficial sources, and because of their often closely restricted circulation, included more confidential information and franker discussion of policy.

The word 'document' has been defined for the purposes of this book as a state paper or paper prepared within the government service for government use.

ACKNOWLEDGEMENTS

It is a great pleasure to express appreciation of the help I have had from Dr. E. E. Mason of Birkbeck College in preparing this book for the press. Dr. H. A. Will of Royal Holloway College kindly read the Introduction for me, and several of the documents came to my attention through his work and that of the late Dr. A. Cariss. I should like to thank also Dr. L. B. L. Crook for comment.

At the Public Record Office I experienced the prompt courtesy and efficiency I have always found there. The staff of the Institute of Commonwealth Studies, London, could not have helped me more. Miss I. G. Ellis assisted me a great deal in the early stages of preparing the book, and Miss A. T. Myles also gave valued help. I am very grateful to both. The book is dedicated to my sister Margaret, who upholds me with love and loyalty.

Transcripts of Crown-copyright records in the Public Record Office appear by permission of the Controller of H.M. Stationery Office.

ABBREVIATIONS

C	British Parliamentary Paper
Cd	Command Paper Number
Cmd	
Cab.	Public Record Office Cabinet series
C.O.	Public Record Office Colonial Office series
C.P.	Cabinet Paper
F.O.	Public Record Office Foreign Office series
Hansard 3s.	Hansard's Parliamentary Debates
4s.	Third, Fourth, Fifth series
5s.	
P.P	British Parliamentary Papers
P.R.O.	Public Record Office, Chancery Lane, W.C.2
P.R.O. C.	Public Record Office Charter series

INTRODUCTION

Between 1880 and 1932 the Commonwealth and Empire grew in size by military conquest, as by the addition of the Transvaal and Orange Free State; it grew by the declaration of protectorates as over south-east New Guinea and the southern Solomon Islands, permissively by the activities of chartered companies such as the British South Africa Company, and by the acceptance of League of Nations mandates. With the growth in size came growth in population. The Commonwealth and Empire gained new resources sometimes of a value beyond ready measurement, as with the Rand gold mines. These new resources ranged from the agricultural and pastoral potential of East Africa to the trade of north Borneo. The years also saw the development of resources already under British sovereignty, and growth in trade.

These years brought change in the title of the monarch and an increase in the Imperial activities of the Royal Family. Queen Victoria's jubilees were made the occasion of the first two Colonial Conferences and King Edward VII's coronation the third. The British Parliament approved the re-wording of the royal title in 1901 and again in 1927 to clarify the authority of the Crown. The duty to appear on major state occasions took members of the Royal Family far afield, as when the Duke of York visited Australia in 1901 (XII, 3) and 1927. Reference to allegiance to the Crown as the central bond of empire was a feature of the Balfour declaration of 1926. The prerogative or statutory powers of the King to disallow laws passed by the parliaments of self-governing colonies had not been exercised for many years by the time the Balfour committee looked into the question in 1926, although other functions of the Crown, such as granting leave of appeal, continued while varying in application with the Dominion concerned.

Growth came also in constitutional activity. The practice of assembly of Imperial representatives evolved from the monarch's jubilees, and with it appreciation of the value of recurrent consultation. Delegates agreed that regular discussion should replace intermittent exchange of views, so indicating the belief within the self-governing colonies that Imperial membership served their interests as well as those of Great Britain. When the Imperial Conference, meeting in theory at regular

intervals, evolved from the Colonial Conference (I), a permanent
secretariat serviced its affairs. Appreciation dawned early, especially
in India, of the value of these conferences to air grievances and seek
redress. Representatives of India brought forward the status of Indians
in British territories abroad as an Imperial issue (II, III).

Before the war constitutional evolution included the inception of
the Committee of Imperial Defence (IV), and during the war the summoning of the Imperial War Cabinet (II) extended the practice of
consultation. After the war the British Government further continued
this practice by calling the Imperial Economic Conference of 1923
(III, 4), which recommended continuance of the Imperial Shipping
Committee and some association of Dominion and Indian representatives in the work of the Imperial Communications Committee. The
Imperial Economic Committee on which all Commonwealth and
Empire governments were represented was established as a result
of the Economic Conference of 1923. In 1925 a West Indian conference
in London accepted the principle of a standing West Indian conference
with a constitution modelled on the Imperial Conference (III, 6).

Readiness to meet the considerable expense of overseas representation was a slow growth. The decision in 1879 to appoint a High
Commissioner for Canada at London was not followed by Australia
or New Zealand for many years. When the Imperial Conference
decided in 1926 that the Governor-General no longer represented
the British Government (III, 6), it agreed to propose increased British
representation in the Dominions in addition to the Governor-General,
and the first British High Commissioner was appointed, at Ottawa,
in 1928. Diplomatic appointments to foreign countries by the Dominions came after the first world war; when the minister for the Irish
Free State took up his post at Washington in 1924, he was the first
Dominions minister to do so.

Growth in status by the Dominions in the field of foreign relations
was a feature of the post-war years. This was most apparent in their
entry into the League of Nations as original members, their separate
representation at international negotiations, separate signature of
international treaties and approval or non-approval of ratification
by their own parliaments. A further aspect of the growth of status was
the acceptance of mandates by some Dominions (III, 6), with consequent accountability to an international commission. The Irish
Free State attempted to advance its status without success, when the
British Government refused to agree that the Anglo-Irish treaty was
a document of international standing.

Within the self-governing colonies in these years, constitutional activity was greatest in Australia where the voluntary federation of six colonies was inaugurated in 1901 (XII, 3). An unharmonious merger appeared in South Africa in the Union of 1910 (IX, 10). A change of constitutional status by a new form of document, namely a treaty, occurred when the Irish Free State became a restricted Dominion in 1922.

Constitutional advance in the tropical dependencies was most marked in Ceylon after 1910 (XI, 4). The concession of elected members in the Ceylon legislative council in that year was followed in 1931 by limited internal self-government in a form new to the Empire. Ceylon was the first Asian territory of the Empire to receive universal adult suffrage.

The restoration of some elected members to the Jamaica legislature in 1884, and the grant of the first elected members to Mauritius in 1885, brought pressure for constitutional advance elsewhere, especially as the spread of literacy and better communications increased study of radical movements within and outside the Empire, and of the constitutions of British colonies with self-government. Travel and education abroad invigorated constitutional debate, especially in Ceylon.

This constitutional advance was not always sustained; retrogression came in Jamaica in 1899, for example, when Chamberlain instructed the Governor to restore the official majority on the grounds that the existing system had failed as a working compromise. On the other hand the first elected members in the history of British West Africa were granted to the Nigerian legislative council in 1922.

There was a great increase in constitutional complexity in the dependent Empire in these years. The Colonial Office juggled with nominated official and unofficial members, and elected members, in the legislative councils of territories where they were promoting constitutional advance in response to demand. Between 1880 and 1932 there was an increase in the number of constitutions intermediate between the purest form of Crown Colony government with an official majority in an entirely nominated legislative council, and representative government where a majority of the legislative council was elected. The motives were to extend political experience and participation of non-officials in ordinance-making, partly with the hope of increasing attention to welfare in the dependent territories. The decisions did not always arise from paternalism, but were often a response to internal unrest as in Ceylon and Mauritius.

The growth in administrative activity and the significance of the

functions of the Colonial Office were recognised by the creation of the
Dominions Department of that office in 1907 (I, **6, 7**), and the Domi-
nions Office in 1925 with a Secretary of State for Dominion Affairs
(III, **6**). Parliamentary and permanent heads of the Colonial Office
also became more active in overseas travel. Joseph Chamberlain's
visit to South Africa in 1902 was the first to a part of the Empire by a
Secretary of State while in office. Major Wood's visit in 1921–2 as a
Parliamentary Under-Secretary was the first of its kind to the West
Indies (VI, **4**). Amery sent W. Ormsby-Gore and Sir S. Wilson to
Africa, and himself visited the Dominions while in office. Thus
acquaintance increased with both personalities and conditions abroad.
The advisory committee on native education in tropical Africa
which the Duke of Devonshire set up in the Colonial Office early in
the nineteen twenties, further illustrates administrative activity (III, **6**).

Acquaintanceship with the natural resources and potentialities
of the Commonwealth and Empire grew. Almost immediately on
taking office, Joseph Chamberlain initiated an enquiry into this field.
The British Government used the device of Royal Commissions both
to meet an immediate need, as with the West Indies commission of
1897 (VI, **2, 3**), and for stock-taking purposes, as in 1912 with the Royal
Commission on Empire resources and trade. They sought to promote
trade by inaugurating the Trade Commissioner service in 1908
(II, **3**).

The years between 1880 and 1932 saw much transfer of population
within the Commonwealth, especially of people from the British
Isles to the Dominions. This was not always a consistent outward
movement, for at some times of depression after the first world war
more emigrants returned to Britain than left during the year. The inter-
settlement of Commonwealth communities increased, as Indian immigration continued into the twentieth century, particularly to the West
Indies and Mauritius. The Indian communities were responsible for
an increase in political activity in their new homes, especially Kenya.

Extension of inter-colonial consultation, facilitated by better
communications, was a feature of these years. Transfer of experience
continued to be a major function of the officers of the colonial service,
particularly the governors. The Colonial Office promoted conferences
of the governors in East Africa in 1926. Inter-regional consultation in
Nigeria led to amalgamation in 1914 (VIII, **4**). The West Indies held
a conference on trade and shipping with the Canadian Government
at Ottawa in 1925 (III, **6**).

What cohesive factors between 1880 and 1932 held the Commonwealth and Empire together and kept it in being? The answer 'British interests' will only serve if it is interpreted as 'interests of British subjects'. The Dominions accepted consultation in the Colonial and Imperial Conferences, the Committee of Imperial Defence and the wartime bodies, although Canada, Australia, and New Zealand legislated for the inception of their own navies rather than accept Admiralty control except upon the decision of their own parliaments. For the most part they continued to use the British Foreign Office for foreign negotiations.

Tables of trade for these years show how far trade was a Commonwealth matter, though inter-imperial trade was not fostered by Great Britain's tariff policy before the Ottawa Conference of 1932. The British Government did, however, attempt to promote trade by directing the attention of the Empire Marketing Board (III, 6) to the encouragement of scientific research into agricultural problems. Drawing on the 'bank' of skill and experience throughout the Commonwealth continued as a traditional practice, and the conversion of the West Indian Agricultural College into the Imperial College of Tropical Agriculture is an example of the increase in 'credit' (III, 2).

How far may the growth of political radicalism be discerned in the tropical dependencies in these years? It was fed by many springs, chiefly British radicalism and nineteenth-century European nationalism with a 'feeder current' of Irish nationalist doctrine and campaigning methods. The foundation of the Indian National Congress provided a precedent for name, and to some extent, organisation and aspiration. The Ceylon National Congress, for example, dates from 1919; the National Congress of British West Africa from 1920 (VIII, 5–8). Encouragement to African political activity in Kenya was provided by the denial of responsible government to the white settlers and the policy statements of the nineteen twenties and 1930 (X, 5–8). Passive encouragement lay in the British acceptance of the Tanganyika mandate with its explicit moral commitments (X, 4).

Was there moral growth on the part of the British Government in these years, and consistency in the recognition of obligation? There was certainly public acknowledgement of responsibility to administer the Empire on behalf of all its inhabitants. The West India Commission of 1897 wrote:

We have placed the labouring population where it is, and created for it the conditions, moral and material, under which it exists, and we cannot divest ourselves of responsibility for its future, and Chamberlain associated himself entirely with this in the Commons in 1898 (VI, **3a**). Wood in his 1922 report on the West Indies wrote:

> For all this mosaic of humanity the Crown, through the Secretary of State, is in the position of responsible trustee: a responsibility of which it cannot morally divest itself until it is satisfied that it can delegate the charge to hands of not less certain impartiality or integrity than its own (VI, **4**).

In his report in 1919 on amalgamation in Nigeria (VIII, **4**), Lugard stated:

> It is a cardinal principle of British Colonial policy that the interests of a large native population shall not be subject to the will either of a small European class or of a small minority of educated and Europeanised natives who have nothing in common with them, and whose interests are often opposed to theirs.

The 1923 White Paper on Indians in Kenya stated the paramountcy in British policy of African interests (X, **5**), and subsequent White Papers reaffirmed this doctrine (X, **6–8**).

Trusteeship was explicit in the terms of the Tanganyika mandate (X, **4**), the 1929 report on closer union in eastern and central Africa, and the Donoughmore report on Ceylon. The Donoughmore commission wrote:

> His Majesty's Government is the trustee not merely of the wealthier and more highly educated elements in Ceylon but quite as much of the peasant and the coolie, and of all those poorer classes which form the bulk of the population. To hand over the interests of the latter to the unfettered control of the former would be a betrayal of its trust (XI, **4**).

The Gold Coast Concessions Ordinance of 1900 and the Belfield report of 1912 on land alienation in the Gold Coast and Ashanti embody the principle of trusteeship for native rights over land and the produce of the land. Ormsby-Gore in reporting on his visit to West Africa in 1926 remarked regarding labour:

> The British Government have again and again laid down that under no circumstances will they undertake to provide compulsory labour for private profit in any British Dependency.

A growth in the feeling of responsibility for public welfare is apparent in the Donoughmore report, a feature of which is concern for the backward state of social and industrial legislation in Ceylon. A new feature in British policy is the introduction proposed in that report of a democratic franchise in a tropical dependency as a basic corrective for this, a recommendation acted on by the British Government. Once they introduced a democratic franchise in Ceylon, it would clearly be difficult to withhold it for very long from other British dependent territories.

British officials displayed concern with other aspects of living conditions in the dependent Empire. Wood drew attention to the high rate of illiteracy in the West Indies, and Ormsby-Gore reported on shortcomings in education in West Africa. Where there were immigrant populations such as the Indians in many dependent territories, the British Government showed concern for their education.

What promises did the British Government make in these years to encourage a rise in political ambition among the non-European inhabitants of the Empire? In 1919 Amery said in the House of Commons:

> ... the ideal towards which we are aiming in the sphere for which the Colonial Office is responsible is the same ideal which is found throughout the rest of our Dominions, the ideal of self-government, the participation of the people of the country, in so far as they are capable of it, in the government of the country (V, 4).

On the other hand Wood's report of 1922 rejected responsible government for the West Indies in the foreseeable future (VI, 4), as did the 1923 White Paper (X, 5) and the 1929 report on closer union of eastern Africa, for Kenya. There is no promise of full internal self-government for Ceylon in the guarded and circumscribed sentences of the Donoughmore report. If the British Government believed it was training non-European peoples for full participation in government and if it were working for this end, it is clear that up to 1932 it could not see the terminal point of this process.

General note

The extracts from the proceedings of the Colonial and Imperial Conferences are very brief. Extensive extracts are to be found in *The Colonial and Imperial Conferences from 1887 to 1937* edited by M. Ollivier (Queen's Printer, Ottawa, 1954). Some extracts are also to be found in *Selected Speeches and Documents on British Colonial Policy, 1763–1917* edited by A. B. Keith (O.U.P.), *Speeches and Documents on the British Dominions, 1918–1931* edited by A. B. Keith (O.U.P.), and *The Development of Dominion Status 1900–1936* edited by R. M. Dawson (Frank Cass, 1965).

There are documents for advanced students and valuable notes in F. Madden (ed.): *Imperial Constitutional Documents 1765–1952* (Blackwell 1953). There are also documents in J. Simmons (ed.): *From Empire to Commonwealth: Principles of British Imperial Government* (Odhams Press 1950).

Irish University Press are to publish a series from the records of the Colonial and Imperial Conferences from 1887 to 1914 from the documents in the Public Record Office, London. The editor of this book is Consulting Editor to the series.

I

CONSULTATION BY CONFERENCE

The Colonial and Imperial Conferences and subsidiary conferences to 1914

1 The Colonial Conference, 1887

The Colonial Conference of 1887 assembled on the occasion of Queen Victoria's Diamond Jubilee at the invitation of E. Stanhope, then Secretary of State for the Colonies. The first meeting was attended by the Prime Minister, Lord Salisbury, and many Cabinet ministers and former ministers, former Secretaries and under Secretaries of State for the Colonies, members of both Houses of Parliament and other eminent men interested in the colonies. Sir Henry Holland was Secretary of State for the Colonies when it met.

SIR H. T. HOLLAND TO THE GOVERNORS OF COLONIES

(Circular.)
Downing Street,
23rd July, 1887

My Lord,
Sir,
    . . . The invitation to the Conference contained in Mr. Stanhope's despatch of the 25th of November last met with a prompt and gratifying acceptance in all quarters. The self-governing Colonies sent as their delegates Ministers, ex-Ministers, or other distinguished Colonists; while, at Meetings in which the Crown Colonies were interested, representative gentlemen, deputed by the local Governments or invited by myself, were present and took part in the proceedings.
    . . . it must be remembered that as the Conference was assembled for consultation and discussion only, its members were not empowered to bind their Governments to any final decisions upon the questions submitted.
    The subject of the organization of Colonial Defence comes first in order of importance. . . .

C 5091

2 The Ottawa Conference, 1894

The Ottawa conference ensued from negotiations between Canada, the Australian colonies and New Zealand. Delegates attended from Cape Colony. The conference met from 28 June to 9 July, 1894. The Canadian Minister of Trade and Commerce, the Hon. Mackenzie Bowell, was elected President. The Marquess of Ripon was Secretary of State for the Colonies at the time of the conference.

REPORT BY THE EARL OF JERSEY ON THE COLONIAL CONFERENCE
AT OTTAWA

The Earl of Jersey to the Marquess of Ripon, London, August 21, 1894
My Lord,
    I have the honour to report that I arrived at Ottawa on the 27th of June, in order to take part, under the authority given to me by your Lordship, in the deliberations of the Colonial Conference appointed to be held there on the invitation of the Canadian Government.
    . . . There was a general feeling of satisfaction and pleasure at the meeting of the Conference, and there were many expressions of loyalty and devotion to the Crown, and of hope that the ties, both of interest and affection, between the Mother Country and her Colonies, and between the Colonies themselves, would be preserved and strengthened.
    . . . the meeting of the Conference suggested some references to the races which are united under the British flag.
    The Chief Justice of the Cape commented on the two-fold character of the population of his Colony, and on the union which is being more and more cemented between the English and the Dutch. He was followed by the Canadian Premier, who bore striking evidence to the loyal conduct of the French-speaking Canadians, and by the Leader of the Opposition in Canada, M. Laurier—a gentleman of the French-speaking race, educated and trained, as he observed, on French systems—who expressed in the warmest terms the loyalty and gratitude to the British Crown of that important portion of the Canadian population.
    I may also remark that the visit of the Australian delegates to Canada impressed them forcibly with the advantages which accrue from the federation of neighbouring provinces. Strong expression was given to this feeling by several of the delegates. . . . I think it is safe to say that

the visit of the Australian delegates to Canada will give an impetus to the movement, and that the knowledge acquired of the details and working of the Dominion Constitution will be of great service to them in considering how federation can be effected in Australia.

On more than one occasion an indication of united Australasian opinion was lacking, and this, to a certain extent, made it impossible for the Conference to be as definite in its conclusions as was desirable upon those points which involved united Australasian support. In the event of its being considered advisable to carry out the resolutions agreed upon, this want of cohesion for the development of Australasian interests will stand in the way and may cause indefinite delays.

. . . I should, perhaps, record my conviction that the sense of connexion and cohesion between the various parts of the Empire has been of late years steadily growing stronger. The great discretion which has been observed at home in connexion with the Colonies has inspired, and is continually augmenting, a feeling of confidence in, and respect for, the Mother Country which is commercially and politically beneficial.

. . . The discussions were substantially confined to the three subjects specified by the Canadian Government when inviting the Conference, viz., the construction of a sub-marine cable from Vancouver to Australia, the establishment of a quick mail service between Great Britain and Australasia viâ Canada, and the trade relations of the Colonies with Great Britain and with one another. . . . [A series of resolutions on trade relations were passed.]

It was clearly the opinion of all the Colonial delegates that it is desirable that the Colonies represented should make arrangements with one another, and, if possible, with Great Britain, which would give British an advantage over foreign products, and that for this purpose any statutory or treaty provisions which stand in the way should be removed. It was felt by the delegates that, so far as might be possible, British subjects should take what they have to import from their own kindred rather than from foreign states. . . .

. . . no support was given to the idea which has been mooted that power should be given to the Colonial Governments to enter into commercial treaties with foreign powers independently of the Imperial Government, and it is obvious that it stands quite apart from the proposal in favour of inter-colonial arrangements. . . .

The resolutions relate to trade and the assistants to trade, but a spirit runs through them the significance of which should not be ignored. Whilst they embody the views of business men, anxious to advance commerce, and of statesmen desirous of developing their countries, quite as distinctly do they show that the self-governing principle is in harmony with the Imperial instinct.

. . . The Mother Country is asked to help in keeping clear the channels between her Colonies and herself, so that the flow of trade may be increased and the feeling of kinship uninterrupted. Never, perhaps, in our Empire's history has such an opportunity presented itself. The 'passionate sentiment' of Canada, as Sir John Thompson so well described it, and the hopeful attachment of the growing Colonies of Australasia and the Cape, turn eagerly at this time to the Mother Country for some sign of her regard for their development.

Their leading statesmen appreciate the value of the connexion with Great Britain, and the bulk of their population is loyal. It is within the power of Great Britain to settle the direction of their trade and the current of their sentiments for, it may be, generations. Such an opportunity may not soon recur, as the sands of time run down quickly. There is an impatience for action which would be tried by delay, and most sadly disappointed by indifference to the proposals which are now brought forward. . . .

C 7553

3   British Cabinet memorandum on the Ottawa Conference

Lord Jersey's Report on the Inter-colonial Conference held at Ottawa last summer has been issued as a Parliamentary paper and is in the hands of all the members of the Cabinet. I therefore desire to bring the questions dealt with in that Report under the notice of my colleagues in order that we may be in a position, when Parliament meets, to state the course which we intend to take with regard to them. . . .

The third resolution advocates the adoption by this country of a system of differential duties in favour of the colonies and *vice versâ*. I do not suppose that the Cabinet would think of abandoning our Free Trade policy in the manner thus proposed, involving, as such a step would, the whole doctrine of Fair Trade. . . . it is clear from Lord Jersey's account of the discussion that the supporters of the resolution themselves had no expectation that the Imperial Government would accept it. I strongly advise its rejection.

. . . I will merely add that the Conference was, from a general point of view, a decided success; that an excellent spirit was exhibited throughout its discussions. . . . It is very important that, whatever may be the ultimate decision of the Cabinet upon the questions raised at Ottawa, the friendly and loyal spirit evinced by the Conference should be met with as much consideration and sympathy as the subjects to be dealt with admit.

RIPON

26th December, 1894

Cab. 37/37/46

4 The Colonial Conference, 1897

The Secretary of State for the Colonies, Joseph Chamberlain, invited the premiers of the self-governing colonies to take part in celebrating the sixtieth anniversary of Queen Victoria's accession, and proposed that they meet for informal discussion. On 24 June 1897 the Prime Ministers of Canada, New South Wales, Victoria, Queensland, South Australia, Western Australia, Tasmania, New Zealand, Cape Colony, Newfoundland and Natal met at the Colonial Office. Chamberlain opened the proceedings.

. . . The commercial relations of the United Kingdom and the self-governing Colonies were first considered, and the following resolutions were unanimously adopted:

1. That the Premiers of the self-governing Colonies unanimously and earnestly recommend the denunciation, at the earliest convenient time, of any treaties which now hamper the commercial relations between Great Britain and her Colonies.
2. That in the hope of improving the trade relations between the mother country and the Colonies, the Premiers present undertake to confer with their colleagues with the view to seeing whether such a result can be properly secured by a preference given by the Colonies to the products of the United Kingdom.

Her Majesty's Government have already given effect to the first of these resolutions by formally notifying to the Governments concerned their wish to terminate the commercial treaties with Germany and Belgium, which alone of the existing commercial treaties of the United Kingdom are a bar to the establishment of preferential tariff relations between the mother country and the Colonies. From and after the 30th July 1898, therefore, there will be nothing in any of Her Majesty's treaty obligations to preclude any action which any of the Colonies may see fit to take in pursuance of the second resolution. . . .

On the question of the political relations between the mother country and the self-governing Colonies, the resolutions adopted were as follows:

1. The Prime Ministers here assembled are of opinion that the present political relations between the United Kingdom and the self-governing Colonies are generally satisfactory under the existing condition of things.

    Mr. Seddon[1] and Sir E. N. C. Braddon[2] dissented.

2. They are also of opinion that it is desirable, whenever and wherever practicable, to group together under a federal union those colonies which are geographically united.

    Carried unanimously.

3. Meanwhile, the Premiers are of opinion that it would be desirable to hold periodical conferences of representatives of the Colonies and Great Britain for the discussion of matters of common interest.

    Carried unanimously.

Mr. Seddon and Sir E. N. C. Braddon dissented from the first resolution because they were of opinion that the time had already come when an effort should be made to render more formal the political ties between the United Kingdom and the Colonies. The majority of the Premiers were not yet prepared to adopt this position, but there was a strong feeling amongst some of them that with the rapid growth of population in the Colonies, the present relations could not continue indefinitely, and that some means would have to be devised for giving the Colonies a voice in the control and direction of those questions of Imperial interest in which they are concerned equally with the mother country.

It was recognised at the same time that such a share in the direction of Imperial policy would involve a proportionate contribution in aid of Imperial expenditure, for which at present, at any rate, the Colonies generally are not prepared.

. . . The question of the Treaty with Japan was brought before the Conference, but, with the exception of Queensland, Newfoundland, and Natal, the Premiers declared that they were not prepared to abandon their former attitude with regard to the Treaty, to which they did not desire to adhere.

They also, with the exception of the Premier of Newfoundland, stated that they did not wish the Colonies they represented to become

---

[1] Prime Minister of New Zealand.   [2] Prime Minister of Tasmania.

parties to the Convention in regard to Trade with Tunis now being negotiated with France.

On the question of the legislative measures which have been passed by various Colonies for the exclusion of coloured immigrants a full exchange of views took place, and though no definite agreement was reached at the meeting, as the Premiers desired to consult their colleagues and Parliaments on the subject, Her Majesty's Government have every expectation that the natural desire of the Colonies to protect themselves against an overwhelming influx of Asiatics can be attained without placing a stigma upon any of Her Majesty's subjects on the sole ground of race or colour.

. . . The subject of the future Administration of British New Guinea, the Solomon Islands and the New Hebrides was introduced, but no decision was arrived at upon it.

July 31, 1897

C 8596

5   The Colonial Conference, 1902

The British Government decided to take advantage of the presence in London of the premiers of self-governing colonies in connexion with King Edward VII's coronation to discuss with them the political and commercial relations of the Empire and its naval and military defence. The Secretary of State for the Colonies, Joseph Chamberlain, opened the proceedings, which were attended by the Prime Ministers of Canada, the new Commonwealth of Australia inaugurated in 1901, New Zealand, Cape Colony, Natal and Newfoundland.

The Secretary of State for the Colonies:

. . . our paramount object is to strengthen the bonds which unite us, and there are only three principal avenues by which we can approach this object. They are: Through our political relations in the first place; secondly, by some kind of commercial union. In the third place, by considering the questions which arise out of Imperial defence. . . .

. . . in my opinion, the political federation of the Empire is within the limits of possibility. I recognise as fully as anyone can do the difficulties which would attend such a great change in our constitutional system. I recognise the variety of interests that are concerned: the immense disproportion in wealth and the population of the different members of the Empire, and, above all, the distances which still separate them, and the lack of sufficient communication. These are difficulties which at one time appeared to be, and indeed were, insurmountable. . . .

. . . His Majesty's Government, while they would welcome any approach which might be made to a more definite and a closer union, feel that it is not for them to press this upon you. The demand, if it comes, and when it comes, must come from the Colonies. If it comes it will be enthusiastically received in this country.

. . . The first thing we have to do . . . is to consider how far we can extend the trade between the different parts of the Empire—the reciprocal trade.

Our first object then, as I say, is free trade within the Empire. . . . But when I speak of free trade it must be understood that I do not mean by that the total abolition of Customs duties as between different parts of the Empire . . . whenever Customs duties are balanced by Excise duties, or whenever they are levied on articles which are not produced at home, the enforcement of such duties is no derogation whatever from the principles of Free Trade as I understand it. If, then, even with this limitation, which is a very important one, which would leave it open to all Colonies to collect their revenues by Customs duties and indirect taxation, even if the proposal were accepted with that limitation, I think it would be impossible to over-estimate the mutual advantage which would be derived from it, the stimulus to our common trade and the binding force of the link which such a trade would certainly create.

Cd 1299

6 Lyttelton[3] despatch about the future organisation of Colonial Conferences, 1905

A. Lyttelton to the Governors of the self-governing colonies, April 20, 1905

11. It will be observed that these Conferences have, step by step, assumed a more definite shape and acquired a more continuous status. Their constitution has lost the vagueness which characterized the assembly of 1887. The Conferences now consist of the Prime Ministers of the self-governing Colonies, together with the Secretary of State for the Colonies, assisted, when the subjects of the discussion make this advantageous, by other high officials of the United Kingdom and the Colonies.

[3] A. Lyttelton was Secretary of State for the Colonies.

12. Again, the first three Conferences met in connection with the presence of the Colonial Representatives in London incidental to important Imperial celebrations. But by the Resolution passed at the last Conference . . . future meetings will be at prescribed intervals, and will be solely for the transaction of business. It may therefore be said that an Imperial Council for the discussion of matters which concern alike the United Kingdom and the self-governing Colonies has grown into existence by a natural process. In the opinion of His Majesty's Government it might be well to discard the title of 'Colonial Conferences', which imperfectly expresses the facts, and to speak of these meetings in future as meetings of the 'Imperial Council'. They desire, without pressing it, to make this suggestion for the consideration of the Colonial Governments.

13. The Secretary of State for the Colonies would represent His Majesty's Government. India, whenever her interests required it, would also be represented. The other members of the Council would be the Prime Ministers of the Colonies represented at the Conference of 1902, or, if any Prime Ministers should be unable to attend, Representatives appointed for that purpose by their Governments.

The permanent body of the Imperial Council would be thus formed, but, as in 1902, their consultations could be assisted, when necessary for special purposes, by other Ministers belonging either to the Imperial or to the Colonial Governments.

14. Upon these points His Majesty's Government would be glad to have the opinion of the Colonial Governments. It would probably be desirable that the future composition of the Imperial Council should be one of the subjects for discussion at the approaching ordinary Conference to be held in the summer of 1906.

15. His Majesty's Government doubt whether it would be wise or necessary to give by any instrument to this Council a more formal character, to define more closely its constitution, or to attempt to delimit its functions. The history of Anglo-Saxon institutions, such as Parliament or the Cabinet system, seems to show that an institution may often be wisely left to develop in accordance with circumstances and, as it were, of its own accord, and that it is well not to sacrifice elasticity of power of adaptation to premature definiteness of form. There is every reason for confidence that the meetings of the Imperial Council (if this name prove to be acceptable to the Colonial Governments) will promote unity both in sentiment and action of the States which, together with the Crown Colonies and Dependencies, constitute the British Empire, and it may be said, without exaggeration,

that upon this unity the peace and welfare of a large part of the world depend.

16. His Majesty's Government now desire to make a suggestion to which they attach considerable importance, for the consideration of the Colonial Governments.

17. It is obvious that the Prime Ministers of the Colonies, when they come to London for these meetings, cannot remain there for long, on account of their important duties at home. It is therefore desirable that subjects which they may agree to discuss should be as much as possible prepared beforehand by a body on which they would be represented, and should be presented to them in as concise and clear a form and with as much material for forming a judgment as possible.

In questions of defence this work is already done by the Imperial Defence Committee, on which also His Majesty's Government desire to obtain from time to time the presence of Colonial Representatives. The present proposal relates, therefore, not to defence questions, but to those of a civil character. . . .

23. Both in the United Kingdom and in the Colonies, when questions arise in regard to which Governments and Parliaments require more light and knowledge before taking action, it is usual to appoint Royal Commissions or Departmental Committees to inquire into the subject and to suggest solutions. His Majesty's Government desire to submit for consideration the proposal that His Majesty should be advised to appoint a Commission of a more permanent kind to discharge the same functions in regard to questions of joint concern. The Commission would only act upon references made either by the Imperial Council, at their meetings, or, at any time, by His Majesty's Government together with one or more of the Colonial Governments. Its functions would be of a purely consultative and advisory character, and would not supersede but supplement those of the Colonial Office. The Commission might be constituted at first for a term of years, and then, if it were found to be useful and successful, it could be renewed. The Commission would, it is proposed, consist of a permanent nucleus of members nominated, in a certain proportion, by His Majesty's Government and the Colonial Governments, but there should be power to the Commission to obtain the appointment of additional members, when necessary, for the purpose of making special inquiries. The persons appointed by the several Governments to be permanent members of the Commission would no doubt be men of business or of official experience, and their remuneration would rest with the Governments which they respectively represented.

24. The Commission should have an office in London, as the most convenient centre, and an adequate secretarial staff, the cost of which His Majesty's Government would be willing to defray. It would probably be convenient that the Secretary of the Commission should also act as Secretary to the Imperial Council when it met. He would be responsible for keeping all records both of the Council and the Commission. . . .

Cd 2785

Mr. Lyttelton to the Governors of the Self-Governing Colonies, November 29, 1905

(Telegram.)
. . . in deference to the views expressed by the Government of the Dominion of Canada it seems to be desirable to postpone further discussion of these matters until the meeting of the next Conference. . . .

Cd 2785

7 The Colonial Conference, 1907

The Colonial Conference of 1907 met at the Colonial Office on 15 April, and the Prime Minister of the United Kingdom opened it. The Secretary of State for the Colonies Lord Elgin was chairman, and Prime Ministers attended from Canada, Australia, New Zealand, Cape Colony, Natal and the Transvaal.

The following Resolutions were unanimously agreed to by the Conference, except where otherwise stated:

I

CONSTITUTION OF THE IMPERIAL CONFERENCE

That it will be to the advantage of the Empire if a Conference, to be called the Imperial Conference, is held every four years, at which questions of common interest may be discussed and considered as between His Majesty's Government and His Governments of the self-governing Dominions beyond the seas. The Prime Minister of the United Kingdom will be *ex officio* President, and the Prime Ministers of the self-governing Dominions *ex officio* members, of the Conference. The Secretary of State for the Colonies will be an *ex officio* member of the Conference and will take the chair in the absence of the President. He will arrange for such Imperial Conferences after communication with the Prime Ministers of the respective Dominions.

Such other Ministers as the respective Governments may appoint will also be members of the Conference—it being understood that, except by special permission of the Conference, each discussion will be conducted by not more than two representatives from each Government, and that each Government will have only one vote.

That it is desirable to establish a system by which the several Governments represented shall be kept informed during the periods between the Conferences in regard to matters which have been or may be subjects for discussion, by means of a permanent secretarial staff, charged, under the direction of the Secretary of State for the Colonies, with the duty of obtaining information for the use of the Conference, of attending to its resolutions, and of conducting correspondence on matters relating to its affairs.

That upon matters of importance requiring consultation between two or more Governments which cannot conveniently be postponed until the next Conference, or involving subjects of a minor character or such as call for detailed consideration, subsidiary Conferences should be held between representatives of the Governments concerned specially chosen for the purpose.

II

COLONIAL REPRESENTATION ON THE COMMITTEE OF IMPERIAL DEFENCE

That the Colonies be authorised to refer to the Committee of Imperial Defence, through the Secretary of State, for advice any local questions in regard to which expert assistance is deemed desirable.

That whenever so desired, a representative of the Colony which may wish for advice should be summoned to attend as a member of the Committee during the discussion of the questions raised.

III

GENERAL STAFF FOR THE SERVICE OF THE EMPIRE

That this Conference welcomes and cordially approves the exposition of general principles embodied in the statement of the Secretary of State for War, and, without wishing to commit any of the Governments represented, recognises and affirms the need of developing for the service of the Empire a General Staff, selected from the forces of the Empire as a whole, which shall study military science in all its branches, shall collect and disseminate to the various Governments military information and intelligence, shall undertake the preparation of schemes of defence on a common principle, and, without in the least interfering in questions connected with command and administration, shall, at the request of the respective Governments, advise as to the training, education, and war organisation of the military forces of the Crown in every part of the Empire.

IV

EMIGRATION

That it is desirable to encourage British emigrants to proceed to British Colonies rather than foreign countries.

That the Imperial Government be requested to co-operate with any Colonies desiring immigrants in assisting suitable persons to emigrate.

Cd 3523

8 British Admiralty memorandum on defence, 1909

On the 16th March of this year statements were made on the growing strength of foreign navies by the Prime Minister and the First Lord of the Admiralty on the introduction of the Navy Estimates for 1909–10.

On the 22nd March the Government of New Zealand telegraphed an offer to bear the cost of the immediate construction of a battleship of the latest type and of a second of the same type if necessary. This offer was gratefully accepted by His Majesty's Government. On the 29th March the Canadian House of Commons passed a resolution recognising the duty of Canada, as the country increased in numbers and wealth, to assume in a larger measure the responsibilities of national defence, and approving of any necessary expenditure designed to promote the speedy organisation of a Canadian naval service in co-operation with and in close relation to the Imperial Navy. On the 15th April Mr. Fisher, the Prime Minister of the Australian Government, telegraphed that, whereas all the British Dominions ought to share in the burden of maintaining the permanent naval supremacy of the Empire, so far as Australia was concerned this object would be best attained by the encouragement of naval development in that country. (On Mr. Deakin succeeding Mr. Fisher as Prime Minister a further telegram was sent on the 4th June, offering the Empire an Australian 'Dreadnought', or such addition to its naval strength as may be determined after consultation in London.)

In view of these circumstances, His Majesty's Government considered the time was appropriate for the holding of a Conference to discuss afresh the relations of the Dominions to the United Kingdom in

B

regard to the question of Imperial defence, and on the 30th April sent an invitation to the Defence Ministers of the four Dominions and the Cape Colonies to attend a Conference under the terms of Resolution 1 of the Conference of 1907, to discuss the general question of the naval and military defence of the Empire, with special reference to the Canadian resolution and to the proposals from New Zealand and Australia.

2. If the problem of Imperial naval defence were considered merely as a problem of naval strategy it would be found that the maximum output of strength for a given expenditure is obtained by the maintenance of a single navy with the concomitant unity of training and unity of command. In furtherance, then, of the simple strategical ideal the maximum of power would be obtained if all parts of the Empire contributed, according to their needs and resources, to the maintenance of the British Navy.

3. It has long been recognised that in defining the conditions under which the naval forces of the Empire should be developed, other considerations than those of strategy alone must be taken into account. The various circumstances of the oversea Dominions have to be borne in mind. Though all have in them the seeds of a great advance in population, wealth, and power, they have at the present time attained to different stages in their growth. Their geographical position has subjected them to internal and external strains, varying in kind and intensity. Their history and physical environment have given rise to individual national sentiment, for the expression of which room must be found. A simple contribution of money or matériel may be to one Dominion the most acceptable form in which to assist in Imperial defence. Another, while ready to provide local naval forces, and to place them at the disposal of the Crown in the event of war, may wish to lay the foundations upon which a future navy of its own could be raised. A third may think that the best manner in which it can assist in promoting the interests of the Empire is in undertaking certain local services not directly of a naval character, but which may relieve the Imperial Government from expenses which would otherwise fall on the British Exchequer.

4. The main duty of the forthcoming Conference as regards naval defence will be, therefore, to determine the form in which the various Dominion Governments can best participate in the burthen of Imperial defence with due regard to varying political and geographical conditions. Looking to the difficulties involved, it is not to be expected that the discussions with the several Defence Ministers will result

in a complete and final scheme of naval defence, but it is hoped that it will be found possible to formulate the broad principles upon which the growth of Colonial naval forces should be fostered. While laying the foundations of future Dominion navies to be maintained in different parts of the Empire, these forces would contribute immediately and materially to the requirements of Imperial defence.

5. In the opinion of the Admiralty, a Dominion Government desirous of creating a navy should aim at forming a distinct fleet unit; and the smallest unit is one which, while manageable in time of peace, is capable of being used in its component parts in time of war. . . .

R. McK.[4]

Admiralty, July 20, 1909

Cab. 37/100/98

9   The Conference on Empire defence, 1909

A statement was made in the House of Commons by the Prime Minister, the Right Honourable H. H. Asquith, M.P., on 26th August, in these terms:

The Conference, which has just concluded its labours, was convened under the terms of Resolution I. of the Conference of 1907. In the invitation sent by His Majesty's Government at the end of April to the Governments of the Dominions, it was stated that the object of the Conference would be to discuss the general question of Naval and Military Defence of the Empire, with special reference to recent proposals from New Zealand and Australia, and to the Resolution passed on 29th March by the House of Commons of the Dominion of Canada. It was further stated that the Conference would be of a purely consultative character, and that it would be held in private. It follows that all Resolutions come to and proposals approved by the Conference which has now been held must be taken, so far as the delegates of the Dominions are concerned, to be *ad referendum*, and of no binding force unless and until submitted to their various Parliaments.

I should add, in special reference to the delegates from South Africa, that they did not feel themselves in a position, in regard to either naval or military defence, to submit or to approve positive proposals until the Union of South Africa was an accomplished fact. With this preface I will briefly summarise the main conclusions of the Conference in regard, first to Military, and next to Naval, Defence.

4 R. McKenna was First Lord of the Admiralty.

Proposals for the Development of the Imperial General Staff

1. His Majesty's Government, in December, 1908, submitted to the Governments of the Over-sea Dominions proposals in regard to the formation of an Imperial General Staff. These proposals have now been accepted in principle. Local conditions in each Dominion are so dissimilar, and differ so widely from those which obtain at home, that it is felt that, having accepted the principles, it now lies with the Governments oversea to take the next step, and to put forward the proposals they advocate for giving practical effect to the scheme in their respective countries.

Cd 4948

10 The Imperial Conference, 1911

The first Imperial Conference was attended by the Prime Ministers of Canada, Australia, New Zealand, the Union of South Africa and Newfoundland.

RESOLUTIONS

The Following Resolutions were Unanimously Agreed To by the Conference, except Where Otherwise Stated

I

Consultation of Dominions as to International Agreements
affecting them.

That this Conference after hearing the Secretary of State for Foreign Affairs cordially welcomes the proposals of the Imperial Government, viz.: (a) that the Dominions shall be afforded an opportunity of consultation when framing the instructions to be given to British delegates at future meetings of the Hague Conference, and that Conventions affecting the Dominions provisionally assented to at that Conference shall be circulated among the Dominion Governments for their consideration before any such Convention is signed; (b) that a similar procedure where time and opportunity and the subject matter permit shall, as far as possible, be used when preparing instructions for the negotiations of other International Agreements affecting the Dominions.

II

Declaration of London. [The Commonwealth of Australia abstained from voting]

That the Conference, after full consideration and debate, approves the ratification of the Declaration of London.

VII
Emigration

Having heard the interesting and explanatory statement from Mr. Burns,[5] resolved, That the present policy of encouraging British emigrants to proceed to British Dominions rather than foreign countries be continued and that full co-operation be accorded to any Dominion desiring immigrants.

XIX
Commercial Treaties

That His Majesty's Government be requested to open negotiations with the several Foreign Governments having commercial treaties which apply to the overseas Dominions, with a view to securing liberty for any of those Dominions which may so desire to withdraw from the operation of the Treaty without impairing the Treaty in respect of the rest of the Empire.

XX
Royal Commission as to Natural Resources and Improvement of Trade of the Empire

That His Majesty should be approached with a view to the appointment of a Royal Commission representing the United Kingdom, Canada, Australia, New Zealand, South Africa, and Newfoundland, with a view of investigating and reporting upon the natural resources of each part of the Empire represented at this Conference, the development attained and attainable, and the facilities for production, manufacture, and distribution; the trade of each part with the others and with the outside world, the food and raw material requirements of each and the sources thereof available, to what extent, if any, the trade between each of the different parts has been affected by existing legislation in each, either beneficially or otherwise, and by what methods consistent with the existing fiscal policy of each part the trade of each part with the others may be improved and extended.

Cd 5745

---

[5] President of the local government board.

II

CONSULTATION BY CONFERENCE DURING THE FIRST WORLD WAR

The Imperial War Cabinet and the Imperial War Conference

When he became British Prime Minister in December 1916, Lloyd George invited Dominion governments to take part in 'a series of special and continuous meetings of the War Cabinet in order to consider urgent questions affecting the prosecution of the war. . . .' The first session of the body which became known as the Imperial War Cabinet was held early in 1917. This and later meetings generally speaking were attended by representatives of all Dominion governments and the government of India, and members of the British War Cabinet. There were also meetings of an Imperial War Conference dealing mostly with problems of imperial policy not directly concerned with the war.

In November 1918 the Imperial War Cabinet began its last session, discussing the forthcoming peace negotiations and Dominion representation at the peace conference. When the Paris conference began in January 1919, it was decided that Canada, Australia, South Africa, New Zealand and India should have their own delegates. During the peace negotiations representatives of Great Britain, the Dominions and India formed the British Empire Delegation to decide a common policy at the conference.

1 The British Government proposal for an Imperial Conference

The Imperial War Cabinet, 20 December 1916

2. The Secretary of State for India[1] drew the attention of the War Cabinet to the omission of India from the approval given for the despatch of a telegram in the Prime Minister's name to the Governors of the self-governing Dominions, in Minute 2 of the previous day's meeting.

The War Cabinet decided that Mr. Chamberlain should draft a

[1] A. Chamberlain.

telegram to the Viceroy in corresponding terms to that approved by the Cabinet and printed in the minute quoted.

3. With reference to the statement made by the Prime Minister in his speech at the House of Commons on the 19th December that His Majesty's Government propose to summon an Imperial Conference to place the whole position before the Dominions and to take counsel with them as to further action, the Prime Minister informed the Cabinet that he proposed to ask the Dominions to send representatives as soon as possible.

Mr. Chamberlain raised the question of India being represented on the Conference, and asked that His Majesty's Government would give the most favourable consideration to the question when the Conference was held. He pointed out the immediate and continued contributions of troops and war material made by India from the very beginning of the war, and the consequent claim for representation.

The War Cabinet approved in principle that India should be represented on the Conference by the Secretary of State, accompanied by such *adjoints* as each different matter might demand, but considered that the whole question was one of such importance that it required further discussion, and that the Secretary of State for the Colonies should be present.

The Secretary was instructed to ask Mr. W. H. Long[2] and Mr. A. Chamberlain to draft the notification to be sent on the subject, for discussion on Saturday, the 23rd December.

Cab. 37/161/46

2   The nature and composition of the wartime meetings

(a) *The Imperial War Cabinet, 22 December 1916*

7. With reference to the conclusion of the meeting held on the 20th December (War Cabinet 12), the Secretary of State for the Colonies reported that he had already taken action to notify the Prime Ministers of the Dominions as to the proposal made by the Prime Minister in his speech on the 19th December for an Imperial conference. He had seen the Prime Minister of New Zealand and Sir Joseph Ward, who had agreed to postpone their departure. He had

[2] Secretary of State for the Colonies.

also ascertained that any difficulty which might be raised by the inclusion of representatives of India could be surmounted by treating this as a special War Conference, and [3]*not as a meeting of the ordinary Imperial Conference*, the constitution of which could only be modified by the unanimous consent of the Conference itself. There were difficulties arising from the domestic situation, about the attendance of several of the Prime Ministers, which might possibly make it necessary for them to send trusted colleagues.

[3]*It was generally agreed that the invitation should be, not to an ordinary Conference, but to attend the War Cabinet for the discussion of urgent matters arising out of the war.* This, it was urged, would fit in with the sentiments of the Dominion representatives, who had been far more impressed and influenced by the meetings of the Committee of Imperial Defence which they had attended in 1911, and at which the foreign policy and defence of the Empire had been fully discussed, than by [3]*the ordinary proceedings of Imperial Conferences.*

It was considered that the invitation should be so framed as to make clear that it was for the purpose of a specific series of special meetings, and that there was no intention of trying to keep the Dominion representatives permanently in London as members of the War Cabinet.

Stress was also laid on ascertaining the views of the Dominions as to the terms on which they could assent to peace. Serious disappointment had been felt by the Dominions at the very inadequate fulfilment hitherto of the promise given early in the war that they should be consulted, and there was a fear on their part that they might be asked to make a sacrifice of their conquests in order to make it easier for His Majesty's Government to fulfil its pledges to Belgium or France.

The status of the Indian representatives was raised by the Secretary of State for India, and after some discussion it was agreed that there could be no ground for objection on the part of the Dominions to the presence of the Secretary of State as the Indian representative, with assessors selected by him in consultation with the Government of India, whose views could be invited at the meetings.

Telegrams for transmission to the Dominions and India by the

[3] NOTE.—The Secretary of State for the Colonies did not agree that the passages in italics represented the decision of the War Cabinet, and considered that the following more correctly represented the decision arrived at: For the first passage, 'not as an ordinary session of the Imperial Conference'; for the second passage, 'an invitation should be sent to the Prime Ministers of the Dominions to attend special sessions of the Cabinet'; and, for the third passage, 'occasional attendance at meetings of the Cabinet, or even of the Imperial Conference'.

Secretary of State for the Colonies and the Secretary of State for
India were drafted and, after discussion, agreed to. (Appendix I.)

It was decided that the telegrams should be sent on Sunday, the
24th December, and communicated to the press on the same day
for publication on Tuesday, the 26th December.

8. The Secretary of State for the Colonies intimated that he would
endeavour to ascertain the views of the Dominions on the German
peace overtures before a public statement was made by the Prime
Minister embodying the answer of the Allies. He expressed the hope
that no definite public pronouncement should be made as regards
the note without some consultation with the Dominions. The Prime
Minister assented.

APPENDIX I

Proposed Amended Telegram to Self-governing Dominions

I Wish to explain that what His Majesty's Government contemplate
is not a session of the ordinary Imperial Conference, [but a special
War Conference of the Empire. Further], they invite your Prime
Minister to attend a series of special and continuous meetings of the
War Cabinet in order to consider urgent questions affecting the prosecution of the war, the possible conditions on which, in agreement with
our Allies, we could assent to its termination, and the problems which
will then immediately arise. For the purpose of these meetings your
Prime Minister would be regarded as a member of the War Cabinet.

In view of the extreme urgency of the subjects under discussion,
as well as of their supreme importance, it is hoped that your Prime
Minister may find it possible, in spite of the serious inconvenience
involved, to attend at an early date, not later than the end of February.
While His Majesty's Government earnestly desire the presence of your
Prime Minister himself, they hope that if he sees insuperable difficulty
he will carefully consider the question of nominating a substitute,
as they would regard it as a serious misfortune if any Dominion were
left unrepresented.

Telegram from Secretary of State to Viceroy, dated December 22, 1916
(Secret.)

With reference to announcement made by Prime Minister in House
of Commons last Tuesday, I have to explain that what His Majesty's
Government contemplate is not a session of the ordinary Imperial
Conference, [but a special War Conference of the Empire. Further],

they are inviting the Prime Ministers of the Dominions to attend a series of special and continuous sittings of the War Cabinet in order to consider urgent questions affecting the prosecution of the war, the possible conditions on which, in agreement with our Allies, we could assent to its termination, and the problems which will then immediately arise. For the purpose of these meetings the Prime Ministers will be regarded as members of the War Cabinet.

His Majesty's Government have invited the Secretary of State for India to represent India at these sittings of the War Cabinet and at the special War Conference. I desire the assistance of two gentlemen specially selected for the purpose in consultation with you, as fore-shadowed in Lord Hardinge's[4] speech in the Legislative Council on the 22nd September, 1915.

It is hoped that the meetings may take place not later than the end of February.

Cab. 37/162/11

(b) *The Imperial War Cabinet, 23 December 1916*

6. With reference to Minute 7 of 22nd December (War Cabinet 15), the War Cabinet further discussed the draft telegram to the Dominions, in view of an amendment suggested by the Secretary of State for the Colonies in the original draft. The effect of this amendment was to invite the Dominions to participation in a special War Conference, which was to be additional to, and separate from, the discussions at the War Cabinet.

(See words enclosed in square brackets in Appendix I of Minutes of War Cabinet 15.)

It was pointed out that the effect of this amendment was contrary to the decision of the Cabinet, which was that participation in the discussions of the War Cabinet was to supersede the idea of a Conference on former lines.

Sir G. V. Fiddes, who attended in the absence of the Secretary of State for the Colonies, said there must have been a serious mis-understanding. The Secretary of State for the Colonies had certainly understood that an Imperial Conference was contemplated, and that this had been promised by the Prime Minister on the 19th December. The Dominions might want to raise other topics besides those suitable to meetings of the War Cabinet. There was also the status of other Dominion Ministers, besides Prime Ministers, or their substitutes,

4 Governor-General of India.

who might wish to attend. It was for these reasons that the Secretary of State had suggested the amendment, in his letter to the Prime Minister of 22nd December, and he had been given to understand that the amendment was approved.

On these points it was agreed—

(1) That the promise of an Imperial Conference was more than covered by participation in the War Cabinet, which would be preferred by the Dominions;

(2) That other topics, if raised by the Dominions, might be discussed outside the Cabinet, but that it was preferable not to invite such discussion, but to confine the invitation to questions of urgency during the war or arising immediately out of its termination;

(3) That other Dominion Ministers could come in as assessors, but that, in any case, it should be left to the Dominions to raise that point. The draft, as finally approved, is printed in Appendix IV.

7. The War Cabinet also approved the telegram by the Secretary of State for India printed in Appendix V.

The War Cabinet considered that, having regard to the great services of India during the war, and the character of the assistants to the Secretary of State for India suggested in his Secret telegram to the Viceroy (Appendix VI), there could not possibly be any tenable objection on the part of the Dominions to the inclusion of a distinguished Native of India among the assistants. It was, however, agreed that it might be convenient to postpone the publication of the names of the representatives for the present.

(Initialled) D. Ll. G.[5]

2, Whitehall Gardens, S.W.
December 23, 1916

APPENDIX IV
Proposed Amended Telegram to Self-governing Dominions

I wish to explain that what His Majesty's Government contemplate is not a session of the ordinary Imperial Conference, but a special War Conference of the Empire. They therefore invite your Prime Minister to attend a series of special and continuous meetings of the War Cabinet in order to consider urgent questions affecting the prosecution of the war, the possible conditions on which, in agreement

[5] The Prime Minister of the United Kingdom D. Lloyd George.

with our Allies, we could assent to its termination, and the problems which will then immediately arise. For the purpose of these meetings, your Prime Minister would be a member of the War Cabinet.

In view of the extreme urgency of the subjects of discussion, as well as of their supreme importance, it is hoped that your Prime Minister may find it possible, in spite of the serious inconvenience involved, to attend at an early date, not later than the end of February. While His Majesty's Government earnestly desire the presence of your Prime Minister himself, they hope that if he sees insuperable difficulty he will carefully consider the question of nominating a substitute, as they would regard it as a serious misfortune if any Dominion were left unrepresented.

APPENDIX V

Telegram from Secretary of State to Viceroy, dated December 24, 1916
(Private.)

With reference to announcement made by Prime Minister in House of Commons last Tuesday, I have to explain that what His Majesty's Government contemplate is not a session of the ordinary Imperial Conference but a special War Conference of the Empire. They are therefore inviting the Prime Ministers of the Dominions to attend a series of special and continuous sittings of the War Cabinet in order to consider urgent questions affecting the prosecution of the war, the possible conditions on which, in agreement with our Allies, we could assent to its termination, and the problems which will then immediately arise. For the purpose of these meetings the Prime Ministers will be members of the War Cabinet.

His Majesty's Government have invited the Secretary of State for India to represent India at these sittings of the War Cabinet, of which for that purpose I shall be a member. I desire the assistance of two gentlemen specially selected for the purpose in consultation with you, as foreshadowed in Lord Hardinge's speech in the Legislative Council on the 22nd September, 1915.

It is hoped that the meetings may take place not later than the end of February.

APPENDIX VI

Telegram from Secretary of State for India to Viceroy, December 23, 1916
(Private and Personal.)

My private telegram of to-morrow regarding Imperial Conference should be made official at once and should be published on Wednesday morning. Until then it should be treated as very secret.

I shall be glad to receive early intimation of your views as to choice of the representatives to assist me. It is important that they should be men of weight and sound judgment and absolutely trustworthy, as I wish to take them, whenever possible, to the sessions of War Cabinet, where most secret matters will be discussed, and to invite them on occasion to speak for India. It is not necessary that either should be an Indian, and Dominions would doubtless prefer that both should be Englishmen, but you will probably feel that it is highly desirable that I should select one Indian.

Cab. 37/162/12

3 The Imperial War Conference, 1917

Meetings of the Imperial War Conference took place between 21 March and 27 April 1917, being held as a rule on alternate days to those of the meetings of the Imperial War Cabinet. The first meeting was opened by the Secretary of State for the Colonies W. H. Long and was attended by the Prime Ministers of Canada, New Zealand, and Newfoundland. General Smuts, Minister of Defence, represented South Africa. India had four representatives. There were no representatives from Australia, as there was a general election in that country.

The Secretary of State for the Colonies Mr. Long regretted the absence of Mr. Hughes. A general election had prevented him from coming. He welcomed the representatives of India, and said:

Yesterday had been held the first meeting of the first Imperial Cabinet which has ever assembled in the Empire. To-day they met at what was the corollary of the Imperial Cabinet, namely the Imperial Conference. They were engaged in a War the greatest and the most terrible in history, and their object both in the Cabinet and in the Conference was to deal with the immediate war problems, with those which will arise on the conclusion of peace, and with any other questions which it may seem desirable to discuss or decide, as being of Imperial interest, without delay.

General Smuts (Minister of Defence, South Africa) observed that only good could come from the inclusion of India in this Conference. ... The Secretary of State for India Mr. A. Chamberlain suggested that questions concerning India's relations with the Empire and affecting vitally her relations with the Dominions and the Empire generally, should come up for discussion, though not necessarily for any decision. He said India had some claim to greater recognition than she had had— she had bled herself white at the beginning of the War to supply the deficiencies of the Empire in troops, arms, and guns. . . .

The conference unanimously agreed to these resolutions:

IV

NAVAL DEFENCE

That the Admiralty be requested to work out immediately after the conclusion of the War what they consider the most effective scheme of Naval Defence for the Empire for the consideration of the several Governments summoned to this Conference, with such recommendations as the Admiralty consider necessary in that respect for the Empire's future security.

V

TRADE COMMISSIONER SERVICE

That the Imperial War Conference welcomes the proposed increase of the Board of Trade service of Trade Commissioners and its extension throughout the British Empire in accordance with the recommendations of the Dominions Royal Commission,[6] and recommends that the Governments concerned should co-operate so as to make that service as useful as possible to the Empire as a whole, especially for the promotion of Inter-Imperial Trade.

VII

REPRESENTATION OF INDIA AT FUTURE IMPERIAL CONFERENCES

That the Imperial War Conference desires to place on record its view that the Resolution of the Imperial Conference of 20th April 1907 should be modified to permit of India being fully represented at all future Imperial Conferences, and that the necessary steps should be taken to secure the assent of the various Governments in order that the next Imperial Conference may be summoned and constituted accordingly.

IX

CONSTITUTION OF THE EMPIRE

The Imperial War Conference are of opinion that the readjustment of the constitutional relations of the component parts of the Empire is too important and intricate a subject to be dealt with during the

[6] On the Natural Resources, Trade and Legislation of Certain Portions of His Majesty's Dominions.

War, and that it should form the subject of a special Imperial Conference to be summoned as soon as possible after the cessation of hostilities.

They deem it their duty, however, to place on record their view that any such readjustment, while thoroughly preserving all existing powers of self-government and complete control of domestic affairs, should be based upon a full recognition of the Dominions as autonomous nations of an Imperial Commonwealth, and of India as an important portion of the same, should recognise the right of the Dominions and India to an adequate voice in foreign policy and in foreign relations, and should provide effective arrangements for continuous consultation in all important matters of common Imperial concern, and for such necessary concerted action, founded on consultation, as the several Governments may determine.

XXI

Imperial Preference

The time has arrived when all possible encouragement should be given to the development of Imperial resources, and especially to making the Empire independent of other countries in respect of food supplies, raw materials, and essential industries. With these objects in view this Conference expresses itself in favour of:

(1) The principle that each part of the Empire, having due regard to the interests of our Allies, shall give specially favourable treatment and facilities to the produce and manufactures of other parts of the Empire.

(2) Arrangements by which intending emigrants from the United Kingdom may be induced to settle in countries under the British flag.

XXII

Reciprocity of Treatment between India and the Self-governing Dominions

That the Imperial War Conference, having examined the Memorandum on the position of Indians in the Self-governing Dominions presented by the Indian representatives to the Conference, accepts the principle of reciprocity of treatment between India and the Dominions and recommends the Memorandum to the favourable consideration of the Governments concerned.

Cd 8566

4 The Imperial War Conference, 1918

Meetings of the Imperial War Conference took place on various dates between 12 June and 26 July 1918, being held, as a rule, on alternate days to meetings of the Imperial War Cabinet.

The Secretary of State for the Colonies Mr. Long, Chairman of the Conference, said:

. . . Resolution No. XXI.[7] recommended, in accordance with the development of Imperial resources: (a) acceptance of the principle that each part of the Empire, having due regard to the interests of the Allies, should give specially favourable treatment and facilities to the produce and manufactures of other parts of the Empire; (b) arrangements by which intending emigrants from the United Kingdom shall be induced to settle in countries under the British flag.

His Majesty's Government are anxious to give the fullest effect possible to the first part of this Resolution, and they appointed a Committee of Ministers last year to consider the best methods and machinery. This Committee has been sitting continuously since its appointment, and is still at work. Reports by the Committee will be laid before the Conference.

As regards emigration, as the result of the recommendations of the Dominions Royal Commission and the Empire Settlement Committee, a Bill, based on their recommendations, has been prepared, and has passed its Second Reading at the House of Commons, setting up a Central Emigration Authority to supervise all matters connected with emigration from the United Kingdom. I am arranging for a copy of this Bill to be circulated to the members of the Conference. . . .

Chairman's Opening Address:
. . . Lastly, I would refer to two Resolutions relating to the position of India. Of these, No. VII. recommended that India should be fully represented at all future Imperial Conferences, and that the necessary steps should be taken to secure the assent of the various Governments . . . when the question was put to them, all the Dominion Governments gladly concurred in this proposal. . . .

The Secretary of State for India Mr. Montagu said:
. . . The loyalty of India to the Person and Throne of King George V.

[7] Of the 1917 Imperial War Conference.

is beyond belief, a living force in the minds of almost every Indian, educated and uneducated. The gratification at the fact that India was given a place in this Conference is one of the most significant features of the past twelve months in India. . . . The war has produced in India not only a new feeling of nationality, but a new feeling of devotion to the British Empire, because of the cause for which it is fighting, and the solid front which it presents to the enemy in the field. . . .

The conference passed these resolutions:

IX
IMPERIAL NEWS SERVICE

The Imperial War Conference is impressed with the importance of securing, (a) that an adequate news service should be available in all parts of the British Empire, and (b) that this service should be supplied through British sources. The Conference requests His Majesty's Government to formulate a scheme with these objects in view, on the lines indicated in the Memorandum prepared by the Minister of Information, and to submit this scheme for the consideration of the Governments represented at the Conference.

XIII
CENTRAL EMIGRATION AUTHORITY

The Imperial War Conference reaffirms the principle laid down by Resolution XXI. of the 1917 Conference, in favour of arrangements being made by which intending emigrants from the United Kingdom may be induced to settle in countries under the British Flag. It is of opinion that the representatives of the Oversea Dominions in the United Kingdom should keep in the closest touch with any new Body established by His Majesty's Government to supervise emigration from the United Kingdom. The Conference is of opinion that the appointment of a Consultative Committee, not to exceed ten members, on which representatives of the Oversea Dominions should sit, to advise any such Body, would afford the best means of co-operation.

XXI
RECIPROCITY OF TREATMENT BETWEEN INDIA AND THE DOMINIONS

The Imperial War Conference is of opinion that effect should now be given to the principle of reciprocity approved by Resolution XXII., of the Imperial War Conference, 1917. In pursuance of that Resolution it is agreed that:

1. It is an inherent function of the Governments of the several communities of the British Commonwealth, including India, that each should enjoy complete control of the composition of its own population by means of restriction on immigration from any of the other communities.

2. British citizens domiciled in any British country, including India, should be admitted into any other British country for visits, for the purpose of pleasure or commerce, including temporary residence for the purpose of education. The conditions of such visits should be regulated on the principle of reciprocity, as follows:

(a) The right of the Government of India is recognised to enact laws which shall have the effect of subjecting British citizens domiciled in any other British country to the same conditions in visiting India as those imposed on Indians desiring to visit such country.

(b) Such right of visit or temporary residence shall, in each individual case, be embodied in a passport or written permit issued by the country of domicile and subject to *visé* there by an officer appointed by, and acting on behalf of, the country to be visited, if such country so desires.

(c) Such right shall not extend to a visit or temporary residence for labour purposes or to permanent settlement.

3. Indians already permanently domiciled in the other British countries should be allowed to bring in their wives and minor children on condition (a) that not more than one wife and her children shall be admitted for each such Indian and (b) that each individual so admitted shall be certified by the Government of India as being the lawful wife or child of such Indian.

4. The Conference recommends the other questions covered by the memoranda presented this year and last year to the Conference by the representatives of India in so far as not dealt with in the foregoing paragraphs of this Resolution to the various Governments concerned with a view to early consideration. . . .

XXIV

Shipping

(1) That in order to maintain satisfactorily the connections, and at the same time encourage commercial and industrial relations, between the different countries of the British Empire, this Conference

is of opinion that shipping on the principal routes, especially between the heart of the Empire and the Oversea Dominions, including India, should be brought under review by an Inter-Imperial Board on which the United Kingdom and the British Dominions and Dependencies should be represented. . . .

Cd 9177

III

THE POST-WAR YEARS TO 1932

1 The Imperial Conference, 1921

The Imperial Conference of 1921 was attended by the Prime Ministers of Canada, Australia, New Zealand and South Africa, the Secretary of State for India and two other Indian representatives.

The conference passed these resolutions:

VI IMPERIAL DEFENCE
(a) Naval

Several plenary meetings and several meetings of the Prime Ministers alone with the Secretary of State for India, were devoted to considering the Naval Defence of the Empire, and the following Resolution was adopted:

> That, while recognizing the necessity of co-operation among the various portions of the Empire to provide such Naval Defence as may prove to be essential for security, and while holding that equality with the naval strength of any other Power is a minimum standard for that purpose, this Conference is of opinion that the method and expense of such co-operation are matters for the final determination of the several Parliaments concerned, and that any recommendations thereon should be deferred until after the coming Conference on Disarmament.

In addition, a number of useful consultations took place between the Admiralty and the Representatives of the several Dominions and India, at which were discussed such matters as the local co-operation of each Dominion in regard to the provision of oil tanks, local naval defence, etc.

(b) Military and Air Defence

A discussion took place on the Military and Air Defence of the

Empire, and the views of the General and Air Staffs on the principles which should be adhered to in order to ensure co-operation in these matters were laid before Ministers. . . .

VII IMPERIAL COMMUNICATIONS
(c) *Shipping*

. . . A Resolution was also adopted to the effect that, pending the constitution of a permanent Committee on Shipping, the existing Imperial Shipping Committee should continue its inquiries. . . .

IX POSITION OF BRITISH INDIANS IN THE EMPIRE

. . . the following Resolution was adopted:

The Conference, while reaffirming the Resolution of the Imperial War Conference of 1918, that each community of the British Commonwealth should enjoy complete control of the composition of its own population by means of restriction on immigration from any of the other communities, recognizes that there is an incongruity between the position of India as an equal member of the British Empire and the existence of disabilities upon British Indians lawfully domiciled in some other parts of the Empire. The Conference accordingly is of the opinion that in the interests of the solidarity of the British Commonwealth, it is desirable that the rights of such Indians to citizenship should be recognized.

The representatives of South Africa regret their inability to accept this resolution in view of the exceptional circumstances of the greater part of the Union.

The representatives of India, while expressing their appreciation of the acceptance of the resolution recorded above, feel bound to place on record their profound concern at the position of Indians in South Africa, and their hope that by negotiation between the Governments of India and of South Africa, some way can be found, as soon as may be, to reach a more satisfactory position.

X EMPIRE SETTLEMENT AND MIGRATION

. . . the following Resolution was finally adopted by the Conference:

The Conference having satisfied itself that the proposals embodied in the Report of the Conference on State-Aided Empire Settlement are sound in principle, and that the several Dominions are prepared, subject to Parliamentary sanction and to the necessary financial arrangements being made, to co-operate effectively with the

United Kingdom in the development of schemes based on these proposals, but adapted to the particular circumstances and conditions of each Dominion, approves the aforesaid Report.

The South African representatives wish to make it clear that the limited field for white labour in South Africa will preclude co-operation by the Union Government on the lines contemplated by the other Dominions. . . .

XIV THE PROPOSED CONFERENCE ON CONSTITUTIONAL RELATIONS
. . . the following resolution was adopted:

The Prime Ministers of the United Kingdom and the Dominions, having carefully considered the recommendation of the Imperial War Conference of 1917 that a special Imperial Conference should be summoned as soon as possible after the War to consider the constitutional relations of the component parts of the Empire, have reached the following conclusions:

(*a*) Continuous consultation, to which the Prime Ministers attach no less importance than the Imperial War Conference of 1917, can only be secured by a substantial improvement in the communications between the component parts of the Empire. Having regard to the constitutional developments since 1917, no advantage is to be gained by holding a constitutional Conference.

(*b*) The Prime Ministers of the United Kingdom and the Dominions and the Representatives of India should aim at meeting annually, or at such longer intervals as may prove feasible.

(*c*) The existing practice of direct communication between the Prime Ministers of the United Kingdom and the Dominions, as well as the right of the latter to nominate Cabinet Ministers to represent them in consultation with the Prime Minister of the United Kingdom, are maintained.

The Secretary of State for the Colonies, Mr. Churchill, made a statement about the colonies and possessions administered directly under the Colonial Office.

. . . As long as the War lasted, practically all the Colonies and Dependencies were very prosperous, but with the arrival . . . of peace a wave of depression has fallen upon almost every one of them so far as their trade is concerned.

. . . the creeping paralysis of depression has spread to almost all the

Colonial industries which flourished during the War . . . we are passing through a stormy period in the economic and commercial life of practically all the Colonies. But if one leaves the immediate difficulties and turns to their great and undoubted wealth and potential capabilities, one cannot help feeling how magnificent is the asset which the British Empire possesses, and of which, pending the development of more responsible and representative forms of government in these Colonies, we in Great Britain and at the Colonial Office are the trustees.

. . . So far as the constitutional developments in the Colonies are concerned, progress has been continuous, and latterly, especially since the War, very rapid. We have every form of government, ranging from benevolent autocracies tempered by Downing Street, to two-Chamber systems, resting upon at least one of the Chambers being fully elected. For instance, the island of Bermuda celebrated its ter-centenary of representative institutions dating from the day when the first general assembly of the islands was made, and therefore can boast a seniority which no existing State in Europe or America can disdain. In Mauritius there was a movement to promote an agitation for a retrocession of the island to France, but this movement has received a decisive check at the recent elections, in which all the retrocessionist candidates have been signally defeated. There has been a strong move-ment in Ceylon for a more popular control over the government of the Colony, following upon the movement which Mr. Montagu and his predecessors have driven forward, fostered, and nourished in India, and a new constitution has been granted which gives a majority in the Legislature to the unofficial element. In the Kenya Colony a new constitution has been granted giving an elective basis for the unofficial members of the Council, instead of the nominated basis which existed hitherto. Uganda has reached such a stage of development that they have a Legislative Council with nominated membership. In Malta a novel experiment has been tried by my predecessor . . . We have arrived at a dyarchical system—two Governments in the island, one elective, dealing with Maltese affairs, and the other dealing with purely military and naval interests.

. . . Rhodesia is a young organization to be trusted with full res-ponsible government. Its population is smaller than Natal, when she obtained responsible government. On the other hand, the settlers are discontented with the present state of affairs. The Chartered Company is passing away, and it therefore has little incentive to spend money on the development of the country. . . . The native question is, of course, a very serious one there . . .

. . . the question of the Indian settlers in some of our Colonies, and no doubt that problem also occurs in South Africa to a certain extent. I think there is only one ideal that the British Empire can set before itself in this regard, and that is that there should be no barrier of race, colour, or creed which should prevent any man by merit from reaching any station if he is fitted for it. At any rate I do not feel able to adopt any lesser statement of principle in regard to the Colonies, but such a principle has to be very carefully and gradually applied because intense local feelings are excited, and there is no doubt that extraordinary social stresses arise when populations are intimately mingled in some of these new countries and brought into severe economic competition. The question reaches its most acute form in Kenya. . . .

Cmd 1474

2   The Imperial Conference, 1923

The 1923 Imperial Conference was attended by the Prime Ministers of Canada, Australia, New Zealand, South Africa, and Newfoundland, two Ministers from the Irish Free State and representatives of India.

In the course of opening speeches, the Prime Minister of Canada, Mr. Mackenzie King said:
. . . Coming from the Dominion of Canada, the close association of the name of our Dominion with that of the new Irish Free State in the Treaty and Constitution makes it a special pleasure to me to have the privilege of meeting at this table the representatives of that State.

The Prime Minister of the Union of South Africa, General Smuts said:
. . . the presence of the Free State here goes to show what the spirit of goodwill can effect. . . . The difficulties which Ireland has passed through and will continue to pass through are difficulties which are not peculiar to her. He [President Cosgrave] will find that many of those questions which confront Ireland are common to the whole Empire. Here he will find help and assistance and sympathy in the consideration of his own problems, and he will find that this Conference, this High Court of our great Commonwealth, is the best forum for the discussion of his problems. . . .
. . . Without any revolutionary departure from the settled fiscal

policy of this country, I think a great deal can be done to foster inter-Empire trade, and I hope that this Conference will register a very great advance in that direction. . . .

. . . It is not only you who wish to re-establish trade—we in the outer Empire want to do the same. We also had our markets in Europe, and they are largely gone. Therefore, even if there were no higher motive than mere self-interest, we should still try our very best to establish conditions of peace and quiet in Europe. . . .

Later in the conference, General Smuts said:

. . . The moral stock of the British Empire, so far as I am informed, is very high in Geneva. I was very much struck by what one of the South African representatives told me on his return from Geneva the other day. He said the most remarkable thing at Geneva is the confidence, the faith, the reliance, which all the small peoples of the world represented there have in the British Empire and in the stand that we are making for justice, fair play, and international honesty. That is a matter of very great importance to us. . . . To my mind there is no doubt that the League is not only a great world interest; it is a British interest too. I thoroughly endorse what Mr. Bruce has said. The more we can make the League a real living force, the less armaments we as an Empire shall require. We cannot rest merely on a military or a naval basis. Something far greater than armaments will be wanted in an Empire as great as ours, and the League seems to me to be a real, substantial, moral reinforcement of our whole position. The more we can strengthen it, the more we can make it a reality, the more secure our position will be, which is not one of military or naval ambitions, but one of peace and social progress in the world. . . .

Statement by the Secretary of State for the Colonies, the Duke of Devonshire:

. . . the Colonies and Protectorates . . . still suffer under the general depression of trade, but . . . taken as a whole, the Colonies are 'pulling through'. The financial position of some of the smaller Colonies is a constant source of anxiety to their Governments and to us, but there are indications that the larger tropical areas for which we are responsible are recovering. Much, however, remains to be done before the trade of the Colonies can be said to be in a satisfactory position, and it is to trade within the Empire that we must look to regain at least part of the ground that has been lost during recent years. Proposals will be placed before the Economic Conference with the object of increasing inter-Imperial trade with our tropical possessions and of fostering their development. But action by Governments alone, however beneficial if rightly directed, is not in itself sufficient and needs to be aided and reinforced by private capital and private enterprise; and this all-important aspect of the question is being explored by an expert Committee under the Chairmanship of Lord Ronaldshay, the late Governor of Bengal. . . .

West Indies
. . . The visit to the West Indies and British Guiana in 1922 of the former Parliamentary Under-Secretary of State (Mr. Edward Wood), who was accompanied by Mr. Ormsby-Gore, gave an impetus to the movement in progress there, as in other parts of the Empire, for constitutional development. At the same time it enabled the Secretary of State to deal with West Indian problems with the aid of the sure knowledge which comes from personal touch with the representatives of every shade of opinion on the spot. . . . It is the fixed policy of the Colonial Office to follow the precedent so successfully established and to take every opportunity of repeating in other parts of the Colonial Empire similar official visits. I have already invited Mr. Ormsby-Gore to pay a visit to the British West African Colonies this forthcoming winter, and I hope that he will be leaving in the middle of December.

As a result of Mr. Wood's visit constitutional reforms are in the course of being carried out in Jamaica, Trinidad, Grenada, St. Vincent, St. Lucia and Dominica.

The economic position of the West Indian Colonies is far from satisfactory. It has been necessary for several Colonial Governments to come to the assistance of their staple industries in order to enable them to tide over a period of grave depression. Both the sugar and the cocoa industries have experienced great difficulties, and the oil industry of Trinidad, from which so much was hoped, has not hitherto come up to the expectations that were formed in regard to it . . .

. . . Another Imperial development which emanates from the West Indies is the recent change in the scope and title of what was formerly known as the West Indian Agricultural College. At a meeting held at the Colonial Office this summer under my Chairmanship it was unanimously agreed that the scope of the College should be Empire-wide, but it was felt that the prospect of obtaining the necessary funds would be gravely impaired if the College retained a title suggesting that it was merely a local institution. It was, therefore, recommended that the title should be changed to the Imperial College of Tropical Agriculture, and our aim is that it should provide for the needs of all tropical dependencies by becoming the chief centre of agricultural research and staff training. . . .

West and East Africa

I now turn to Africa. The British West and East African colonies both in area and population provide our greatest opportunity and the widest scope for sustained development. In those large tropical territories the improvement of communications and the advancement of education are the foundation of moral and material progress. New railway construction is now steadily proceeding in Nigeria, Gold Coast and Kenya, while important harbour works are being carried out at Takoradi in West Africa (Gold Coast) and at Kilindini in East Africa (Kenya). It is also hoped that the last link in the connection by railway of Lake Nyasa with the coast at Beira will soon be undertaken.

Kenya and Uganda

In Kenya political questions have recently overshadowed all others. It has been no easy task to provide an equitable adjustment of the several interests concerned in the political future of the Colony, but, after very careful consideration, the British Government has taken certain decisions which have been made public and which I need not here repeat. . . .

. . . In the administration of Kenya, as in other African Colonies and Protectorates, we regard ourselves as exercising a trust on behalf of the African population. Whatever measures we take must be considered in their relation to that paramount duty. We propose to continue the general policy of moral, economic and intellectual development of the African. Within the limits of their finances the East African Governments will continue, side by side with the great work of the Missions, to do all that is possible for the advancement of the natives. Considerable progress has already been made, and the Uganda Railway Administration is now paying special attention to the training of natives for mechanical work on the railways. It is confidently anticipated that in time mechanical work of this kind and the ordinary clerical work of Government will be carried out by Africans.

Tanganyika Territory

In East Africa we administer, under a mandate issued by the League of Nations last year, a territory larger than any Colony, that of Tanganyika. The country's prosperity depends mainly upon agriculture and it has suffered from the general trade depression, besides having much lee-way to make up owing to the wreckage caused by the War.

Progress is, however, being made, though revival is necessarily slow. Revenue is steadily increasing, and the relations between the native population and the Government are excellent. It has been found possible to make a considerable reduction in the military garrison. The system of administration which has been adopted is to support and supervise, with the least possible interference, the established native authority. It is recognised that, except to a very limited extent, the country is not suitable for European settlement, and this has been recently affirmed by the adoption of a Land Law modelled closely on one which has stood the test of time in the Northern Provinces of Nigeria. 'Compulsory servitude,' which is the same thing as slavery, has been abolished without any of the social disturbance that was dreaded in some quarters, and, I may add, without expense. This was a step which our German predecessors had never ventured to take. We are now able to spend more money on native education—though not so much as I would wish—and also on agriculture, thanks to the liberal assistance afforded by the Empire Cotton Growing Corporation, who regard the Territory as a promising field for development.

Rhodesia

In Rhodesia important constitutional changes are now taking place.

As explained by Mr. Churchill, the position when the last Conference was held in 1921 was that a delegation from Southern Rhodesia was due to arrive shortly in this country to discuss the terms of the future constitution. As the result of this visit, draft Letters Patent providing for the constitution of responsible Government were prepared with a view to submission to the electors in Southern Rhodesia. Subsequently discussions were also held in South Africa between the Union Government and representatives from Southern Rhodesia regarding the alternative policy of entry into the Union.

Following on these discussions, a referendum was held in October of last year on the question whether the territory favoured entry into the Union or the grant of responsible government. The referendum having resulted in a vote in favour of the latter alternative, the new Constitution has accordingly now been completed and came into force this week on the 1st October. Difficult questions which had arisen with regard to the unalienated lands and the rights of the British South Africa Company on the termination of their administration have now been satisfactorily settled by means of agreements which have been arrived at with the Company and the Elected Members of the present Legislative Council of Southern Rhodesia. The settlement with the

Company involves a substantial contribution from Imperial funds in addition to the amount for which the new Administration will make itself responsible. The settlement should be of material assistance to the new Government in the discharge of its responsible task. Under the new Constitution certain powers with regard to native administration are reserved to the High Commissioner for South Africa, but in other respects the people of Southern Rhodesia will have a full control of their Government and administration. In Northern Rhodesia, under the agreement made with the British South Africa Company, the British Government will relieve the Company of the administration on the 31st March, 1924. . . .

Ceylon

. . . In Ceylon the new Constitution granted in 1920, under which the unofficial element in the legislature is given a majority, has . . . worked successfully for three years, although some further modifications of the Constitution are now under consideration. Ceylon's tea and copra trade is flourishing, and there has recently been a substantial improvement in the position of the rubber industry as the result of the measures for the restriction of output undertaken jointly by the rubber-growing Colonies.

Malaya

I am glad to report that the economic depression in Malaya, especially in the two main exports of tin and rubber, would seem to be passing.

The revenue has improved, and the financial stringency, which was especially severe in the case of the Federated Malay States, is to some extent relieved. A large loan of £10,000,000, of which £9,000,000 have already been issued on the London market, has enabled the administration to be carried on and important public works to be proceeded with. The loan has been entirely applied to Federated Malay States purposes, but in order that it might be a trustee security it was found necessary that it should be issued by the Colony of the Straits Settlements, which has re-lent it to the Federated Malay States.

The Colony itself has come through a severe period of adversity without having to borrow for its own purposes.

Hong Kong

The disturbed condition of the neighbouring Chinese province of Kwang Tung and of China generally has naturally had a bad effect on the trade of Hong Kong as a distributing centre for South

China, but in spite of this the trade returns for last year would have shown a considerable increase on those of the previous year had it not been for a very serious strike of Chinese labourers which paralysed the port for several weeks in the spring of 1922. A large scheme is under contemplation at present for an extensive reclamation under-taking, designed to increase the facilities of what is already, from the point of view of tonnage entered and cleared, the biggest port in the world.

Of all parts of the Empire, Hong Kong has probably come through the recent acute period of trade depression with the least loss and suffering. This is due to the fact that, as the entrepôt of South China, she profits from every branch of the huge and varied export trade of China, as well as from its European imports. It is also true that political unrest in China has diverted much wealth and capital to the neighbour-ing British Colony, in which the merchants and well-to-do classes of Chinese have implicit confidence.

Fiji

Fiji has suffered from the loss of the Australian market for its principal export products, namely, sugar and fruit. But thanks to New Zealand, which now takes the bulk of the sugar crop, these islands, which are of great importance to our Imperial position in the Pacific, have passed the worst. . . .

Falkland Islands and Antarctic

. . . the late Captain Scott's Antarctic ship, the 'Discovery', has been purchased on behalf of the Government of the Falkland Islands for employment mainly in research into whaling in the Dependencies of the Colony. . . .

Middle East

This concludes what I have to say to-day about the Colonies and Protectorates, but my survey would be incomplete without some special reference to developments in the Middle East. The supervision of this area, which includes Iraq and Palestine, was assumed by the Colonial Office in the spring of 1921. . . .

Cmd 1988

3   The Imperial Conference discussion on foreign relations, 8 October, 1923

A note by the Lord President of the Council, 10 October 1923

All the Dominion representatives agreed that what may be called local foreign affairs should primarily be managed by the Dominion concerned. The Dominion Government would of course consult the Foreign Office in respect of the negotiations but how far they were to be guided by it did not clearly appear. The Dominions no doubt somewhat differ on this point. But leaving that detail out of account a generally similar view as to the treatment of local foreign affairs was the extent of the agreement upon the constitutional issues. It is true that both the Canadian and the Australian Prime Ministers considered that their Dominions should not be involved in international complications without the consent of their Governments, but this premise led them to precisely opposite conclusions. Mr. Mackenzie King deduced from this point of departure that Canada generally speaking should have nothing to do either with the decision of foreign policy or with its consequences. Mr. Bruce on the other hand held the view that the Dominions should share in every important decision in a foreign policy which should be the foreign policy of the Empire as a whole. Mr. Massey's opinion was again rather different. He agreed with Mr. Bruce that the Dominions could not escape being committed by decisions of foreign policy and he would be glad to be consulted beforehand so far as possible. But unlike Mr. Bruce he did not think this to be essential, and he was prepared to accept the decisions of Great Britain on foreign affairs and to see her through.

General Smuts made little more than a passing reference to the bare constitutional question. It was I understood in harmony with the position of Mr. Bruce. But General Smuts' full attitude upon the constitutional question is to be inferred from the rest of his speech. To him not only must foreign policy be a function of the Empire, but its right direction is so self-evidently necessary in the interests of the whole that to disinterest himself or South Africa, as Mr. Mackenzie King suggested for Canada, did not occur to him as possible. He approached the subject just as an English Minister might approach it—as entitled to be consulted and to give his judgment upon every issue involved. As to the question whether the present arrangements are sufficient he said nothing beyond the intimation that satisfactory machinery ought to be provided. Mr. Bruce was evidently aware of some of the difficulties which stand in the way of the course he advocates and acordingly it was part of his plan that the Foreign Office should as far as possible employ the machinery of the League of Nations to deal with the less important international questions as they arise.

How far it may be wise to face the issues raised in this discussion on the present occasion may be disputed. It is not easy to steer between the dangerous disinterestedness of Mr. Mackenzie King's position and the cumbrous procedure involved in the idea of Mr. Bruce. On the other hand there may be a greater risk in disappointing men who are already rather disillusioned as to the reality of Imperial Conferences and in meeting issues sharply raised with obstruction or evasion. If anything is to be done—and I think something must be done—what we ought to aim at is machinery which, though of course absolutely equivalent in the case of each Dominion, could be used or allowed to remain dormant according as each Dominion might desire. Then solvitur ambulando. Australia will find how much common action is possible, and Canada will learn how much common action is desirable, and we shall put constraint upon neither one nor the other. I suggest that the only direction in which this can be achieved is by the permanent presence in London of representatives of each Dominion, of the highest standing, as confidential as an Ambassador, but trained in political affairs, who should be consulted by us upon all international issues of Imperial importance, should interpret the mind of their Government, and before decisions are made should act as the channel of communication between them and ourselves so that a community of view may be established.

    . . . it remains true that the dissatisfaction of the Dominion Governments with our conduct of foreign affairs is a fact of real importance. We can scarcely leave it there. . . . We must reckon with Empire opinion. . . .

(Intd.) S.[1]

October 10, 1923

Cab. 24/62 C.P. 408(23)

4 The Imperial Economic Conference, 1923

It was decided to adopt the following Resolution:

This Imperial Economic Conference approves the Report of the Committee appointed to consider questions relating to oversea settlement. The Conference endorses the recommendations of the Committee and notes with satisfaction the arrangements as recorded in the Report which have been arrived at, or are in contemplation, with a view to improving the facilities for settlement within the Empire.

    The Conference takes this opportunity of reaffirming its sense of

---

[1] Lord Salisbury.

the importance of the policy of oversea settlement to the well-being of the Empire.

It was agreed that the Scheme recommended by the Committee on Co-operation in Financial Assistance to Imperial Development be adopted. The Report of the Committee reads as follows:

The Committee on Financial Co-operation recommends for adoption by the Conference the following scheme which was submitted to the Committee by the representatives of His Majesty's Government.

The suggestion which the Imperial Government make is that in order to facilitate the anticipation of work which otherwise would not be taken in hand for some years they should give a contribution towards the interest charges on loans raised for capital expenditure of this kind by public utility undertakings (viz., communications, power lighting, water, drainage, irrigation, &c.). These undertakings might be under either public or private control or management.

The assistance would be in respect of expenditure on orders placed in this country and would be applicable only to schemes approved by the Dominion or Central Government concerned and certified by it to be in anticipation of normal expenditure. Payment would be made to the Dominion or Central Government which would be responsible for payment to the ultimate recipient.

It is suggested that the maximum grant should be three-quarters of the interest charges for a period of five years.

In order to qualify for the Imperial contribution a scheme must be accepted by the Imperial Government within the next three years. The approval on behalf of the Imperial Government would be given after consultation with the Treasury, the Colonial or India Office and the Board of Trade.

It would be understood that priority will be given to schemes involving the earliest placing of orders.

It was decided to adopt the following Resolution:

This Imperial Economic Conference, holding that, especially in present circumstances, all possible means should be taken to develop the resources of the Empire and trade between the Empire countries, desires to reaffirm the Resolution on the subject of Imperial Preference passed by the Imperial War Conference of 1917.[2]

[2] See p. 35.

C

It was decided to adopt the following Resolutions:

(i) Commercial Diplomatic and Consular Services.

This Imperial Economic Conference takes note of the offer of His Majesty's Government to place the services of His Majesty's Commercial Diplomatic Officers in foreign countries at the disposal of the Governments of the Dominions and India and of the Colonies and Protectorates in the same way and to the same extent as the services of His Majesty's Trade Commissioners within the Empire are already at their disposal. It notes that His Majesty's Government propose that as regards countries outside of Europe the Governments should utilise direct the services of Commercial Diplomatic Officers or of senior Consular Officers where no Commercial Diplomatic Officers have been appointed, but that communications which it is proposed to address to Commercial Diplomatic Officers in European countries should be transmitted in the first instance to the Department of Overseas Trade.

The Conference, recognising the importance of all possible steps being taken to strengthen the mutual co-operation of the several parts of the Empire in matters of commercial intelligence with a view to the development of Empire trade, welcomes the arrangements proposed by His Majesty's Government.

It also welcomes the offer of the Governments of the Dominions which have appointed Trade Commissioners in countries overseas to make a similar arrangement for the utilisation of those officers by Governments of other parts of the Empire. . . .

[It was decided to adopt the following Resolution] That this Imperial Economic Conference is of opinion:

(1) That the work accomplished by the Imperial Shipping Committee is convincing proof of the wisdom of its establishment, and that it is of the highest importance to the Empire that this work should continue;

(2) That it is, therefore, desirable to maintain the Committee on its present basis, deriving authority from, and responsible to, the Governments represented in the Imperial Conference.

It was decided to adopt the following Resolution:

That in the opinion of this Imperial Economic Conference (Canada dissenting):

(1) It is desirable to establish an Imperial Economic Committee, comprising representatives of the Governments represented in the Imperial Conference, and responsible to those Governments.

(2) The function of the Committee should be to consider and advise upon any matters of an economic or commercial character, not being matters appropriate to be dealt with by the Imperial Shipping Committee, which are referred to it by any of the constituent Governments, provided that no question which has any reference to another part of the Empire may be referred to the Committee without the consent of that other part of the Empire.

It was further decided that in the constitution of the proposed Imperial Economic Committee representation should be allotted to the various constituent Governments as follows:

Great Britain	4 members
Dominions	2 members each
India	2 members
Colonies and Protectorates	2 members

Cmd 1990

5   The British Government on the resolutions of the 1923 Imperial Economic Conference

Extracts from Statement, April 1924

. . . Co-operation in financial assistance to Imperial Development
This Resolution recommends for adoption the proposals put before the Conference for a contribution by His Majesty's Government to interest charges on loans raised in the United Kingdom for capital expenditure on or in connexion with public utility undertakings with the object of accelerating enterprises of Imperial Development which would not otherwise be immediately undertaken. His Majesty's Government endorse these proposals, and legislation to enable effect to be given to them has already been introduced in the present Parliament.

Co-operation for Technical Research and Information
These Resolutions recommend the reorganization of the Imperial Institute and the incorporation with it of the Imperial Mineral Resources Bureau. Since the Economic Conference terminated, certain modifications of the scheme of reorganization have been under discussion.

His Majesty's Government hope to be in a position to introduce the necessary legislation into Parliament at an early date.

Oversea Settlement

This Resolution approves the report of the Committee of the Conference which was appointed to consider Oversea Settlement.

Since the Conference terminated agreements have been made with the Governments of the Dominion of Canada and the Commonwealth of Australia in respect of passages for families, juveniles and women.

His Majesty's Government accept the Resolution and will continue to give effect by administrative action to the policy of Oversea Settlement as embodied in the Empire Settlement Act, 1922.

Commercial, Diplomatic and Consular Services

Under this Resolution it was proposed to place at the disposal of Dominion and Colonial Governments the services of His Majesty's Commercial Diplomatic Officers (or of senior Consular Officers where no Commercial Diplomatic Officers have been appointed) in the same way and to the same extent as the services of His Majesty's Trade Commissioners within the Empire.

The necessary instructions are in preparation for issue to all Diplomatic Missions. . . .

Imperial Shipping Committee

The Resolutions of the Conference warmly commended the work of the Imperial Shipping Committee and recommended its continuance on its present basis. His Majesty's Government appreciate the value of the work of the Committee and readily endorse this Resolution.

Air Communications

These Resolutions recommend the circulation of information throughout the Empire and reciprocal consultation on questions of air development.

His Majesty's Government have under preparation a scheme for the mutual interchange of aeronautical information, and will take steps to keep the other Governments concerned fully informed of developments which may occur in regard to airship services. . . .

Imperial Economic Committee

This Resolution recommends the establishment of an Imperial Economic Committee. His Majesty's Government have already announced in Parliament that they have decided, particularly in view of the fact that the Economic Conference itself did not reach unanimity on the subject, that they cannot support the adoption of the recommendation.

Cmd 2115

6   The Imperial Conference, 1926

The 1926 Imperial Conference was attended by the Prime Ministers of Canada, Australia, New Zealand, South Africa and Newfoundland, and representatives of the Irish Free State and India. The conference referred all questions on the agenda affecting inter-imperial relations to a committee of Prime Ministers and heads of delegations of which the Lord President of the Council, the Earl of Balfour, was asked to be chairman.

OPENING SPEECH BY THE PRIME MINISTER OF GREAT BRITAIN

Nowhere has the necessity for adjusting the relations between the Governments of the Empire been more conspicuous than in the region of foreign policy. . . .

. . . The problem before us is how to reconcile the principle of self-government in external as well as domestic affairs with the necessity for a policy in foreign affairs of general Imperial concern which will commend itself to a number of different Governments and Parliaments.

That problem we have already gone some way to meet. The first conspicuous demonstration of the changes which had taken place in the sphere of foreign affairs was the Imperial War Cabinet of 1917. This was followed by the Imperial War Cabinet of the following year and the Empire Delegation at the Peace Conference. In the seven years that have since elapsed there have been (including the present Conference) three sessions of the Imperial Conference. At the last two Conferences, not only has a common understanding been arrived at as regards the principles which should govern the main issues of foreign policy, but also agreements have been reached on what I may term the administrative side of foreign relations in matters of major importance. I need only refer to the part played by the Conference of 1921 in the discussion which preceded the Washington Disarmament Conference and to the work of the Conference of 1923, first, on the problem of Reparations, which led up to the Agreements reached in 1924, and, secondly, on the question of smuggling off the United States coast, which resulted in the conclusion of the Treaty

for the Regulation of the Liquor Traffic. Apart from meetings of the
Imperial Conference, there have been a number of International Conferences since the war, at which the Dominions have been represented
and have played an important part, in addition to the periodical
meetings of the Assembly of the League of Nations at Geneva, where
there has invariably been close and constant touch between our
respective representatives.

Present System for Diffusion of Information

Side by side with the increase in the opportunities for interchange
of views afforded by personal contact at such Conferences has gone
a continuous increase in the diffusion of information. You will remember that, following on the promise made by Lord Curzon
at the Conference of 1921, copies of all communications of importance
to and from His Majesty's representatives abroad bearing on current
aspects of world politics and on the conduct of foreign affairs are now
sent without delay from London to the Prime Ministers of the Dominions, and day by day they are kept informed by telegram and
despatch of every important development and tendency. . . . The
present Prime Minister of the Commonwealth has supplemented this
system by the appointment in London of a personal liaison officer in
close touch with the responsible authorities in this country. . . .

Resolution of 1923 Conference on Negotiation, &c., of Treaties

A beginning has also been made, on the more formal side, in
indicating the principles which govern our national and international
relationships. I am thinking particularly of the Resolution on the Negotiation, Signature, and Ratification of Treaties which was agreed to
at the Imperial Conference of 1923, and has since been accepted by
all the Governments represented here. It may well be that this Resolution, in the light of experience, now needs clarification and amplifica-
tion in certain ways. But I can say with confidence that its usefulness
has been amply demonstrated in the course of the last three years.

Developments as affecting Defence

In the field of Imperial Defence there has been steady, if unobtrusive,
progress towards improving the facilities for co-operation, if the necessity should unhappily arise. The long-drawn-out controversy of the
early part of this century between the advocates of Dominion Navies
and Dominion contributions to a single Imperial Navy has long since
died away in the natural and inevitable course of constitutional
development. The principle of Dominion Navies is established, and

is not merely accepted, but is whole-heartedly endorsed, by the Admiralty. I take this opportunity of warmly welcoming the step recently taken by India in establishing the Royal Indian Navy. At the end of this year, in accordance with the provisions of the Articles of Agreement of 1921, we shall be entering upon a conference with representatives of the Irish Free State with a view to the undertaking by the Free State of a share in her own coastal defence. A regular system for the interchange of British and Australian cruisers is now in operation. Our Navies, on which we depend in the last resort for our corporate existence, remain—and I venture to say will continue—one of the strongest possible bonds that unite us.

In the land forces also much has been done to facilitate co-operation. At the present time units and formations throughout the Empire are organised in general on similar lines. Broadly speaking, similar patterns of weapons are in use, and a human bond is created by a system of interchange of Officers, and by personal visits of Officers to and from the Dominions.

In the Air arm, whose actual and potential importance is a link between us, not only from the point of view of Imperial Defence, but also from that of Imperial communications, has been strikingly demonstrated by recent long-distance flights; contact and co-operation are being secured by corresponding methods.

In all these services common doctrine in matters of defence is provided for by special facilities for the attachment of Officers to colleges and other technical establishments, and we hope to see this process extended.

. . . The third, and not the least important, head under which the work of the Imperial Conference may be classified is that of Empire Trade and Empire Settlement. One of the most striking of the definite results of recent Conferences has been the institution of a number of joint Imperial bodies, each surveying some particular aspect of the Empire's economic, as opposed to its political, relations. Thus, at this Conference we shall be called upon to consider the valuable work done by the Imperial Shipping Committee and the Imperial Economic Committee. I would refer also to the Imperial Institute, which has recently been reorganised as a result of the work of the Imperial Economic Conference of 1923, with which is now amalgamated the Imperial Mineral Resources Bureau—the latter itself the product of Resolutions of the Imperial War Conferences of 1917 and 1918; also to the advances which have been made since the last Conference in co-operation in research within the Empire; and to the work of successive Conferences on Forestry, one result of which has been the establishment at Oxford University of an Imperial Forestry Institute.

In the sphere of direct trade relations between the different parts of the Empire, the most striking developments of recent years have been the greater realisation of the importance to the Empire of fostering inter-Imperial trade. We in this country may fairly claim to have played our part, from a very early date, by the facilities given in London, both in the raising of loans, and in giving such loans the privileged position of Trustee Securities. From no other source could such large sums have been provided on such favourable terms. I find, for instance, that down to the end of 1925 London had lent to Governments and Municipalities in Canada, Australia, New Zealand, and South Africa more than £850 millions sterling. In spite of the reduction in the wealth of this country and the diminution of its accumulated savings resulting from the World War, and in spite of the heavy consequential drain on our savings for capital expenditure in this country, we have been able, even in the years since the war, to maintain the flow of investments which is so important for oversea development. In addition we took a further step, as the direct result of the special Conference held in the early part of 1921 and of suggestions made by the Dominions' representatives at the subsequent Imperial Conference, in passing the Empire Settlement Act of 1922. The problem of settlement . . . is essentially a problem of co-operation, not only in actual measures directly concerned with migration and settlement, but also in finance and in the marketing of Empire products.

The principle of Imperial preference, which, I gladly admit, was initiated and pressed in the Dominions before the Government of this country recognised its advantages, was first unanimously accepted in its widest sense by the Imperial War Conference, 1917, and the Resolution then passed was re-affirmed in 1923. Substantial results have followed from the preference accorded in the Dominions to Empire goods, and I am confident that the measure of preference which we in this country have been able to afford, even under our very limited tariff system, supplemented as it will be in the future by the operations of the newly established Empire Marketing Board, has increased and will increase the flow of inter-Imperial trade. . . .

Establishment of Dominions Office

I should like to add here a brief reference to . . . the establishment last year of a separate Dominions Office under the supervision of a

Secretary of State for Dominion Affairs. I will leave it to my colleague who holds that office to set forth in greater detail the reasons for that change and the advantages which we hope to see resulting from it. But I should like to say that I believe that this development, whilst not interfering in any way with the personal communications between Prime Ministers on matters of Cabinet importance, which both I and they feel to be of the greatest value, will do much to facilitate the conduct of our relations with the Governments of the Dominions.

Unofficial Relations

. . . Such relations exist in every sphere of our life as a Commonwealth. I need only instance the Empire Parliamentary Association with its reciprocal visits of parliamentary delegations—whose object, as Lord Salisbury recently put it in New Zealand, 'is to bring about, not political union, but a union of hearts and sympathies'; the extent to which advantage is being taken of the facilities provided by our Universities, where during the past year, in round numbers, 1,200 students from the Dominions and over 1,000 from India have pursued their education, without counting large numbers of Law students and students in technical schools and research institutes; the Rhodes Trust, which since its inception has enabled 565 students from the Dominions in addition to 69 from the Colonies to pursue their education at Oxford University; the close connection maintained by the churches; the reciprocal visits of scientific bodies, of press representatives, of farmers, students, scouts and guides, indeed of societies of all kinds; the mutual recognition of professional diplomas in medicine and other branches of science. . . .

. . . The President of the Board of Trade Sir Philip Cunliffe-Lister advised the conference that the Imperial Economic Committee was established in March, 1925: They have already presented four reports. In their first report they made recommendations as to the allocation of the annual grant for the promotion of trade in Empire produce and as to the identification of Empire goods, besides recommending the establishment of the body which has now been set up as the Empire Marketing Board.

In the remaining three reports, they examined and made recommendations regarding the preparation for market and the marketing of meat, fruit, and dairy produce.

. . . The object of the Marketing Board is to advise upon the detailed application of the £1,000,000 grant. I have no doubt that, wisely administered, that grant can be made of enormous value in increasing the sales of many Empire products, and in improving, by research, efficiency in production, transportation, and marketing. This grant is being made by the Home Government in lieu of certain preferences which we proposed at the Imperial Economic Conference, and to which we were precluded from giving effect. I think it is almost certain that, operating over a wide field, it will be of more value in increasing sales of Empire produce than the limited preferences for which it was substituted.

At the same time we have done not a little in the extension of preference. We have enacted those preferences which were within our power, and, what is probably more important still, we have, under the Finance Act of this year, stabilised the preferences for a period of 10 years, by providing that, so long as the duty is maintained at a rate exceeding or equal to the present preferential rebate, the full pecuniary value of the preferences shall not be reduced.

These and other examples have done much to win general approval for preference as a permanent feature in our limited tariff. And it is right that this should be so, when we remember that over £100,000,000 worth of our exports enjoy preference in different parts of the Empire. . . .

Statement by the Secretary of State for Dominion Affairs

Establishment of Dominions Office

Mr. Amery: The Prime Minister has already referred to the alteration in our machinery here for communication and consultation with our partner Governments in the Empire which has been effected by the creation of a separate Secretaryship of State for Dominion Affairs. . . .

. . . the case on constitutional and sentimental grounds for a clearer differentiation between Dominion affairs and Colonial affairs was reinforced by very practical considerations. Both on the Dominions side, and on the Colonial side, the volume of work had grown out of all recognition, and had become far more than the existing machinery could efficiently cope with.

The time had come for a change. . . . That change has taken the form of the creation of a Secretaryship of State for Dominion Affairs and a Dominions Office entirely separate and distinct from the Secretaryship of State for the Colonies and the Colonial Office. The full extent and significance of the change has been to some extent obscured by the fact that for reasons of practical convenience the new Dominions Office is still housed in the Colonial Office, and that the two Secretaryships of State are for the time being vested in the same individual. But the union is, if I may use the term, a personal and not an organic union, and there is nothing to preclude the appointment of two separate Ministers to the two offices, or the combination of the Secretaryship of State for Dominion Affairs with some other office than the Colonial Secretaryship. . . .

. . . the Imperial Economic Committee began its work, I think at the beginning of last year, and it has since produced four reports. The first was a very interesting general report, dealing with the work of marketing Empire food produce, followed by a meat report, a fruit report, and a dairy produce report . . . in the word 'Empire' the Imperial Economic Committee has always included this country, this Home Dominion, as an essential part of the Empire . . . the Imperial Economic Committee has done extraordinarily valuable work. The results of their work have become available in various ways for the business community in every part of the Empire—we have taken measures to secure a fairly wide circulation of its reports—and for the Governments, and further also for the Government of this country in connection with the particular machinery it has set up in the Empire Marketing Board. The existence of that machinery and of a substantial fund, which can be spent on purposes for assisting marketing, has undoubtedly added a great deal to the concrete value of the work of the Imperial Economic Committee. . . .

. . . Empire Marketing Grant

From that I come to the Empire Marketing Board. That is something that has arisen entirely independently since the Conference of 1923. . . . At the Imperial Economic Conference in 1923, the British Government was prepared to offer certain preferences to Empire products . . . we found that, while the greater part could be carried out, there were some of them, involving additional food duties, which were so widely held to be inconsistent with the pledges which the Prime Minister had given at the Election, that it would have been regarded as a breach of faith with the electorate to carry them out in that form. On the other hand, it was equally felt in the Cabinet here that it would be a breach of faith to the rest of the Empire if they were not carried out in some form, and the conclusion we came to was this. We calculated what would have been the equivalent value to the Empire of the preferences if they had been put into force, and we decided that this amount should be devoted through a fund to the furtherance of the marketing of Empire produce.

. . . Tropical Agriculture Research and Training
. . . The first really important Institution to be started, the Imperial College of Tropical Agriculture in Trinidad . . . has now been in existence for two or three years and has already done immensely valuable work. Its graduates are already holding important posts in the agricultural world all over the Empire and in some foreign countries. . . . There is in the tropical Empire one other institution of great importance . . . the Amani Institute, which the Germans established in what is now Tanganyika Territory.

[Mr. Amery continued[2]] . . . the total trade of the Colonies last year—and for this purpose I am excluding the immense in and out entrepôt trade of Hong Kong—was over £500,000,000. Moreover, this trade has expanded enormously in recent years. In 1905 the total exports from the United Kingdom to the Colonies amounted to £18,000,000; in 1913 the figure was £47,000,000, and in 1925, £60,000,000; our imports from the same territories were £19,500,000 in 1905, £40,000,000 in 1913, and £81,000,000 in 1925, i.e., a quadruple increase within twenty years, and, even after making all reasonable deductions for change in money values, it is a greater increase of trade proportionately than our trade with any other part of the Empire . . .

[Mr. Amery referred to] the meeting in London last summer of a West Indian Conference of all the main Colonies, continental as well as insular, round the Caribbean. They met in London because London, under present shipping conditions, is the most convenient centre for the West Indies. They met for the purpose of considering the establishment, and drafting the constitution, of a standing body to deal with their common affairs. For the first time in their history these Colonies, entirely on their own initiative and not under any instruction from the Colonial Office, met under the roof of that Parliament from which so many of their assemblies are directly descended, in order to face the problem of how to get together in order to help each other and to be able to deal more effectively in trade and other matters with the outside world. That Conference was a complete success. They unanimously accepted the principle of a standing West Indian Conference . . . they expressly modelled their constitution upon that of the Imperial Conference. If I may quote from their own Report—'The West Indian Conference is a purely advisory body, with no executive powers, meeting at regular intervals and performing for its constituents functions analogous to those which the Imperial Conference

[1] As Secretary of State for the Colonies.

performs for the Empire as a whole.' . . . This Conference is to meet alternately in London and in the West Indies. . . . It is to have a permanent and travelling Secretariat.

Dealing with the general relations of the West Indies, another important event in their history in recent years has been the Conference on Trade and Shipping which they held with the Government of the Dominion of Canada at Ottawa in 1925. There have been shipping and trade relations, a system of mutual preference, between Canada and the West Indies for a good many years past. Those relations were strengthened and developed by the Conference held between those Colonies and Canada in 1920. . . .

Mr. Amery summarised the problems of tropical Africa under the four heads of transport, scientific agriculture, public health, and native education: I have already referred . . . to the re-opening of the Institute at Amani. I may mention that an Agricultural Conference attended by agricultural officers and specialists, such as entomologists, mycologists, and so on, from most of the Governments, both British and foreign, in East and West Africa, met at Nairobi this year, representatives of the Empire Cotton Growing Corporation also being present. I hope that this and similar conferences will accomplish much in developing scientific agricultural work in Africa.

. . . Our increasing interest in [public health] is reflected in the steadily increasing provision made in the budgets of all the Governments concerned and in the increase in the medical and sanitary staffs employed under all these Governments. . . . We were greatly helped in [native education] from the United States. The Phelps-Stokes Fund of New York organised two Commissions, one going to West Africa in 1921 and a second to East and South Africa in 1924, to enquire into the whole question of native education . . . they have gone out with an entirely impartial mind and have produced reports which have been very useful to us, and which give results coinciding very closely with the results of the discussions of the Advisory Committee on Native Education in Tropical Africa which was set up in the Colonial Office by the Duke of Devonshire immediately after the last meeting of the Imperial Conference. Our whole endeavour now is to substitute for a purely literary education, not suited to the needs of the natives, a type of education more adapted to their mental aptitude—a type of education which, while conserving as far as possible all the sane and healthy elements in the fabric of their own social life, will also assist their growth and evolution on natural lines and enable them to absorb more progressive ideas; it aims, above all, at the building up of character on the part of the native, at giving him an understanding of his own environment, at making him useful in his own environment rather than at giving him the kind of education which is really only suitable in the environment of a country like Great Britain.

. . . Throughout West Africa we have endeavoured as far as possible to govern indirectly, in fact to use, instead of establishing a direct system of British administration, the native States that existed before, the Emirates of Northern Nigeria or the tribal authorities existing in Southern Nigeria and the Gold Coast, to rule the natives as far as possible, and as far as the conditions and standards of civilised government permit, through their own rulers to whom they are accustomed, in accordance with their own ways and their own traditions. Those methods may, perhaps, in some respects not be as advanced as those which would be introduced if we applied European standards directly, but they are much more suited to the natives; they lead to greater contentment, and I think they pave the way by a natural, though slow, transition to a greater measure of native participation in the government of their own affairs than if all existing institutions were wiped out and the whole thing were put under a bureaucratic, though possibly efficient, white administration.

The economic progress of West Africa in recent years has been remarkable. . . . The total net trade of the West African Colonies amounted to over 41 million pounds sterling in 1923 and over 55 million last year . . .

[The visit of the Prince of Wales to West Africa] aroused everywhere the greatest enthusiasm among all the native populations and among the native chiefs . . . I believe from all the reports I have had from Governors and political officers that the effect of that visit was not only momentary but has been lasting, and has served greatly to strengthen the attachment of these peoples to the conception of a great Empire into which they have come and from which they have already derived enormous benefits. [East Africa] is not like West Africa, a country where only the black man can live . . .

. . . On the other hand, it is not South Africa; it is not a country which can be described as a white man's country in that sense. Only a very small proportion of the total population can ever be a white population. Thus it stands in some way midway between these two types and calls for a policy of its own—what has been described as a dual policy—a policy which regards both its primary trusteeship of the native inhabitants already there and the fact that the main development of their country must come through development in trade, in civilisation, in health, in the progress of the natives themselves, and which, realising that there is room and space there for the establishment of white communities, is prepared to give these white communities every possible encouragement for their healthy development.

Governors' Conference

The first important result [of the Commission which visited East Africa under Mr. Ormsby-Gore's chairmanship] was the meeting of a Conference of the Governors of all these Colonies at Nairobi in February of this year and the establishment there again, in Africa, of something in the nature of a Conference system modelled upon the system of our Imperial Conferences. . . .

Development of Transport

The Ormsby-Gore Commission laid great emphasis on the importance of developing the transport system of East Africa, and particularly the system of railway transport, and in pursuance of its recommendations His Majesty's Government decided at the end of last year that it would guarantee a loan of £10,000,000 for the development of transport—railways, harbours, and roads—the loans to be raised by the various Governments concerned. . . . I hope to get through Parliament within the next few weeks the necessary Bill guaranteeing these loans. . . . As regards the trade of East Africa, the total net trade of East Africa in 1923 was over £17,000,000; 1925 shows that it has been increased to nearly £28,000,000.

Southern Rhodesia

. . . Southern Rhodesia entered upon its career as a self-governing Colony just as the last Imperial Conference was beginning. Since then it has made very marked progress, its revenue and its trade have expanded, and its population is showing as healthy and satisfactory an increase as its limited total would justify. . . .

Ceylon

. . . Ceylon has had a new constitution since 1920, a constitution further amended in 1923, under which the unofficial element in the legislature now has a majority. That constitution has worked smoothly, and under it both the general administration and the economic progress of the Colony are going on most satisfactorily. The total value of the exports from Ceylon in 1925 exceeded £31,000,000, as compared with £22,000,000 in 1923. Tea, rubber, coconuts, and all staple products are in a flourishing condition. The railway system is being extended. Work has been begun on a large hydro-electric scheme which will provide adequate power for industrial development . . . the conversion of the Ceylon University College into a full fledged University is receiving active consideration.

Straits Settlements and Malay States

[In] The Federated Malay States and Singapore . . . you have an instance of what I might call indirect government maintained to its fullest extent. These States are still administered, though with the help of British officials, under the authority and control of the native Sultans, and the manner in which they have been brought into the British Empire, conserving their rights and their traditional dignities, has undoubtedly played a great part in that intense loyalty to the British connection which has throughout animated the rulers and peoples of these States . . . they have offered to assist and accelerate the establishment of the Naval Base at Singapore . . . the general prosperity of Malaya . . . has been remarkable. Its exports increased from £78,000,000 in 1923 to £150,000,000 in 1925—in fact, its exports are the largest in the world per head of population. That has been in no small measure due to the fact that Malaya is one of the world's largest producers of rubber and of tin. . . .

Hong Kong

. . . It is, or was until a few months ago, the largest in-and-out shipping port in the world and had built up an immense trade. Its prosperity at the beginning of last year was unexampled. . . .

Statement by the Australian Prime Minister regarding New Guinea

Mr. Bruce: [In regard to the Australian mandate over New Guinea] It is vital to Australia that this territory of New Guinea should be held by Australia in some way, and in no circumstances should it ever again get into the hands of any foreign Power . . .

Statement by the Prime Minister of New Zealand regarding Western Samoa

Mr. Coates: . . . New Zealand, with the exception of her third interest in the mandate of Nauru, has had only Western Samoa to control under a mandate . . . since New Zealand assumed control, the natives have been granted self-government in relation to their land and customs to an extent immeasurably more than they had hoped for under German rule. . . .

Statement by the South African Prime Minister regarding South-West Africa

General Hertzog: . . . there are about 22,000 to 24,000 Europeans in the country. These Europeans were not satisfied with the system of Government by Proclamation through the Administrator, and the result was that after enquiry the Union Parliament passed an Act whereby a limited form of self-government was given to them.

Cmd 2769

[The 1926 Imperial Conference passed these resolutions:]

Imperial Agricultural Research Conference

The Conference notes with approval the proposal to hold a conference in London in 1927 representative of the organisations of the Empire concerned in agricultural research and its administration, for the purpose of discussing such questions as the extension of co-operation between the organisations; the promotion of join programmes of research; the utilisation of the results obtained; and the training, supply, and interchange of scientific workers.

The Conference urges the respective Governments to give the fullest possible support to the proposed Imperial Agricultural Research Conference.

[*This concerned the Imperial Bureaux of Entomology and Mycology*]

Empire Cotton Growing Corporation

(b) The Conference notes with pleasure the success attending the activities of the Empire Cotton Growing Corporation and commends to the favourable notice of the respective Governments the steps which the Corporation is taking to co-operate with the administrative and agricultural Departments concerned in the promotion of cotton-growing within the Empire.

Empire Marketing Board

(c) The Conference notes with satisfaction the attention given by the Empire Marketing Board, in addition to its other activities, to the encouragement of scientific research into the problems of Empire agriculture; and approves the general principle adopted by the Board, wherever possible, of making financial grants for research conditional on proportionate contributions from other sources.

The Conference, in particular, expresses its cordial approval of the project envisaged by the Board of fostering a chain of research stations situated in appropriate centres in tropical and sub-tropical parts of the Empire, and commends this project to the sympathetic consideration of Governments, institutions, and private benefactors throughout the Empire.

Imperial Institute

(*d*) The Conference approves the steps taken to carry out the
recommendations of the Imperial Economic Conference of 1923
for the reorganisation of the Imperial Institute, and expresses its
satisfaction at the progress which has been made since the reorganisation.

. . . It was generally agreed that the Imperial Economic Committee,
on which all the Governments of the Empire were represented, established as a result of the Economic Conference of 1923, had done admir-
able work in the reports so far compiled, and that the Board established
by His Majesty's Government in Great Britain to administer the Empire
Marketing Grant voted by the Parliament at Westminster provided
a most valuable means of assisting in bringing into practical operation
the improvements which as the result of this Committee's investigations, or from further enquiries, were shown to be desirable. . . .

[The Conference passed these resolutions:]

The Imperial Conference is of opinion that the work of the
Imperial Shipping Committee is of importance to the Empire and
that it is desirable to maintain the Committee on its present basis,[3]
deriving authority from, and being responsible to, the Governments
represented in the Imperial Conference.

The Imperial Conference is of opinion that the Imperial Economic
Committee should continue on its present *ad hoc* basis with the
following general reference:

(1) to complete the series of investigations into the marketing of
Empire foodstuffs in Great Britain, and while this work is
proceeding
(2) to put forward for the consideration of the various Governments concerned (a) a list of raw materials for possible further
marketing enquiries, and (b) suggestions for the preparation
and circulation of brief preliminary surveys, as suggested by
the General Economic Sub-Committee of the Conference,
of any branch of Empire trade and marketing, such preliminary surveys, if the Governments concerned so desire, to be
followed up by further enquiries.

Cmd 2768

---

[3] Tenth Report of the General Economic Sub-Committee.

7   The Imperial Conference, 1930

The 1930 Imperial Conference was attended by the Prime Ministers of Canada, Australia, New Zealand, South Africa and Newfoundland, and representatives of the Irish Free State and India.

XII GENERAL ECONOMIC CONCLUSIONS

It was apparent that all parts of the Commonwealth were united in a common desire that all practicable steps should be taken to promote and develop inter-Imperial trade, and at the Second Plenary Session of the Conference, held on the 8th October, a discussion of great importance took place on the methods to be used to achieve this end. . . .

No statement of policy was made on behalf of His Majesty's Government in the United Kingdom during the Second Plenary Session, but at the meeting of Heads of Delegations on the 13th November, the following statement was made by their representatives:

1. His Majesty's Government in the United Kingdom, believing that the development of inter-Imperial markets is of the utmost importance to the Commonwealth, have declared that the interests of the United Kingdom preclude an economic policy which would injure its foreign trade or add to the burdens of the people; but that their fiscal policy does not preclude marketing propaganda and organisation which will secure valuable opportunities for the consumption of Dominion products in the United Kingdom.

2. His Majesty's Government in the United Kingdom have suggested that the Governments of the Empire should undertake to make forthwith a close examination of the various methods by which each may make the greatest possible contribution to economic co-operation within the Empire with a view to presenting reports to a Conference which, it has been suggested, should be held next year or as soon as the reports are ready.

3. In the meantime His Majesty's Government in the United Kingdom have declared that the existing preferential margins accorded by the United Kingdom to other parts of the Empire will not be reduced for a period of three years or pending the outcome of the suggested Conference, subject to the rights of the United Kingdom Parliament to fix the budget from year to year.

4. His Majesty's Government in the United Kingdom agree to reconstitute the Empire Marketing Board as a body with a fixed minimum annual income, with a provision enabling it to receive

such other contributions from public or private sources as it may be willing to accept, for the purpose of furthering the marketing of Empire products.

5. His Majesty's Government in the United Kingdom agree to the reconstitution of the Imperial Economic Committee on the lines recommended by the Committee of the Conference on Economic Co-operation.

. . . The Report of the Committee on Economic Co-operation . . . together with the views expressed on behalf of the various Governments, were considered at Meetings of Prime Ministers and Heads of Delegations held on the 12th and 13th November.

At the latter Meeting it was decided to recommend the following Resolutions, which were adopted by the Conference:

I The Imperial Conference records its belief that the further development of inter-Imperial markets is of the utmost importance to the various parts of the Commonwealth.

II Inasmuch as this Conference has not been able, within the time limit of its deliberations, to examine fully the various means by which inter-Imperial trade may best be maintained and extended, it is resolved that the Economic Section of the Conference be adjourned to meet at Ottawa on a date within the next twelve months to be mutually agreed upon, when that examination will be resumed with a view to adopting the means and methods most likely to achieve the common aim; provided that this reference is not to be construed as modifying the policy expressed on behalf of any of the Governments represented at this Conference.

III The agenda for the meeting referred to in the previous resolution will be agreed between the several Governments.

Imperial Economic Committee

. . . During consideration of the work of the Imperial Economic Committee, the general question of arrangements for the examination of economic matters of inter-Imperial concern arose. The Committee on Economic Co-operation recommended, and the Conference adopted, the following Resolutions:

I The Conference is of opinion that the Imperial Economic Committee should continue as at present established, but takes note of the desire expressed by His Majesty's Government in the United Kingdom that their representation should be on the same basis as that of other parts of the Commonwealth.

II The Conference is further of opinion that the Chairman of the

Imperial Economic Committee should be elected annually by the Committee from among its own Members, regard being paid to the desirability of rotation.

III The Conference considers that the general reference to the Imperial Economic Committee should be as follows:

(1) to complete the series of investigations into the marketing of Empire foodstuffs in the United Kingdom;

(2) to undertake inquiries into the production for export and the marketing in various parts of the world of the raw materials enumerated in the Fifteenth Report of the Imperial Economic Committee;

(3) to prepare, at the instance of the Governments of the Commonwealth, preliminary surveys of any branch of Empire trade and marketing such as were contemplated in the recommendation of the Imperial Conference of 1926;

(4) to carry out any investigations arising out of recommendations contained in Reports submitted by the General Economic Committee and adopted by the present Conference;

(5) to facilitate conferences among those engaged in particular industries in various parts of the Commonwealth;

(6) to examine and report on any economic question which the Governments of the Commonwealth may agree to refer to the Committee.

Empire Marketing Board

The Committee on Economic Co-operation recommended certain resolutions with regard to the work of the Empire Marketing Board and the Conference adopted them in the following form:

I The Conference, having surveyed the work of the Empire Marketing Board, is satisfied that it is valuable to the Commonwealth as a whole, and recommends its continuance and its extension in certain directions, notably in the spheres of market intelligence, statistical surveys and market promotion.

II The Conference takes note of the Empire Marketing Board's programme of research, involving commitments approaching £2,000,000 from the Empire Marketing Fund, as well as independent contributions by so many Empire Governments. It finds that programme in accord both with the Resolution of the Imperial Conference of 1926 and the policy adopted by the Imperial Agricultural Research Conference of 1927.

III The Conference commends especially that feature of the Board's policy which aims at the concentration and development in the most appropriate centres of scientific team work upon problems of interest to the Commonwealth as a whole, and notes as an example of special promise the recognition and extension of the Onderstepoort Veterinary Research Station as an Empire centre of research in the field of animal health.

IV The Conference also welcomes the facilities provided by the Board for enabling scientific workers to visit different parts of the Empire.

V The Conference is of opinion that if effective advantage is to be taken of the opportunities for co-operative action within the British Commonwealth open to the Board:

(1) The limitation of the Empire Marketing Fund to marketing in the United Kingdom should be removed.

(2) While the amount of its contribution must remain wholly within the discretion of the Parliament of the United Kingdom, it should be recognised that the efficiency of the Board's work and its opportunities for effective planning depend upon a minimum annual income being assured to the Board over a reasonable period.

(3) The Board should therefore be constituted as a body with a fixed minimum annual income, with a provision enabling it to receive such other contributions from public or private sources as it may be willing to accept, for the purpose of furthering the marketing of Empire products.*

* *Note.*—The representatives of the Union of South Africa considered that the Fund was and should remain the concern solely of the Government of the United Kingdom and could not, therefore, agree to paragraph (3) of Resolution V.

XIX Research

Subjects connected with scientific research were considered by a Committee of the Conference comprising senior officers of the research departments of the various Governments of the British Commonwealth, under the Chairmanship of The Right Honourable Lord Parmoor, K.C.V.O., Lord President of the Council.

The position with regard to co-operation in agricultural research may be regarded as generally satisfactory. As the outcome of the recommendations of the Imperial Conference of 1926 and of the Imperial Agricultural Research Conference of 1927, eight agricultural bureaux have been established for the interchange of information in eight branches of agricultural science. Scientific conferences are growing in number and importance. Improvements have been effected in the arrangements for the recruitment and training of agricultural research workers. Investigations have been carried out with the aid of funds provided by the Empire Marketing Board involving team work between research organisations in different parts of the British Commonwealth.

The following Resolutions were passed by the Research Committee on co-operative developments connected with agricultural research:

Results of Imperial Agricultural Research Conference, 1927
(i) The Research Committee of the Imperial Conference note with satisfaction the remarkable growth within the Commonwealth during the last four years of co-operative activity in the field of agricultural research designed to meet the needs to which the Imperial Conference of 1926 drew special attention.

(ii) The Committee welcome the success of the first Imperial Agricultural Research Conference held in London in 1927, and, being satisfied that great benefits accompanied and have followed the holding of that Conference, urge the respective Governments to give their fullest possible support to the second Conference to be held in 1932, and to facilitate the representation of universities and research institutes at that Conference.

Imperial Agricultural Bureaux
In the establishment of the eight Imperial Agricultural Bureaux, financed from a common fund and controlled by a Council of nominees of the Governments of the Commonwealth, the Research Committee of the Imperial Conference find both a notable precedent for action on a true Commonwealth basis and a contribution that is already bearing fruit in the better dissemination of scientific knowledge throughout the Empire.

Research Grants of the Empire Marketing Board
(i) The Research Committee of the Imperial Conference take note of the Empire Marketing Board's programme of research, involving commitments approaching £2,000,000 from the Empire Marketing Fund as well as independent contributions by so many Governments. They find that programme in accord both with the resolution of the Imperial Conference of 1926 and the policy adopted by the Imperial Agricultural Research Conference of 1927.

(ii) The Committee commend especially that feature of the Board's policy which aims at the concentration and development in the most appropriate centres of scientific team work upon problems of interest to the Commonwealth as a whole, and note as an example of special promise the recognition and extension of the Onderstepoort Veterinary Research Station as an Empire centre of research in the field of animal health.

(iii) The Committee also welcome the facilities provided by the Board for enabling scientific workers to visit different parts of the Empire. . . .

Questions referred to the Research Committee by the General Economic Committee of the Conference

The General Economic Committee referred a number of matters to the Research Committee for an expression of opinion on the scientific issues involved, and recommendations were made as follows. . . .

(c) *Imperial Institute*

(i) The Research Committee desire to record their view that the Imperial Institute is specially fitted to discharge its duties as a clearing-house for the collection and dissemination of information relating to the commercial and industrial utilisation of the raw materials, including the mineral resources, of the Empire by virtue of the valuable information and experience accumulated by the staff during the last thirty years, by means of its contacts with technical Government Departments and producers of those materials in the Dominions, India and the Colonies, and by its close association with scientific and technical authorities and with the trades and industries concerned with the different groups of raw materials.

(ii) The Committee recognise that a close degree of co-operation already exists between the Imperial Institute and organisations in the United Kingdom engaged in agricultural and industrial research, and in the promotion of marketing facilities for, and the commercial utilisation of, Empire products, and recommend that in any scheme for the economic development of the resources of the Empire that may emerge as the result of this or of future Imperial Conferences, full advantage be taken of the services the Institute is in a position to render. . . .

Cmd 3717

IV

DEFENCE

Policy making and administrative reorganisation

The principal organ of Imperial co-operation in defence before the first world war was the Committee of Imperial Defence established by Balfour in December 1902. It had its origins in the Colonial Defence Committee of 1878, an inter-departmental committee of officials. This lasted only a year. In 1885 the British Government appointed a standing committee, which continued in existence and became a sub-committee of the Committee of Imperial Defence in 1902. It made proposals on broad principles of Imperial defence.

Lord Hartington, later Duke of Devonshire, was chairman of a royal commission on defence administration. It sat from 1888–90, and recommended a council of service ministers and chief professional advisers under the Prime Minister's presidency. This was the embryo of the Committee of Imperial Defence. Lord Salisbury set up the Defence Committee of the Cabinet in 1895 under the presidency of the Duke of Devonshire.

The Anglo-Boer War of 1899–1902 hastened administrative reorganisation in the Admiralty and War Office, and led the Duke of Devonshire to prepare a memorandum in 1900 on the Defence Committee of the Cabinet.

1 Minute by the Prime Minister[1]

[Dated October, 1895]

1. The normal composition of the Committee of Defence should be as small as possible. I do not think that it should exceed the President, the Secretary at War, the Commander-in-Chief, and the First Lord and First Naval Lord of the Admiralty. This should be the normal body to whom all papers, agenda, &c., should be regularly circulated. But in the course of its deliberations the Committee will have from time to time to consult other members of the Government, the Chancellor of the Exchequer, perhaps the Leader of the House of Commons, the Secretaries of State for Foreign Affairs, for the Colonies and for India.

[1] Lord Salisbury.

These should not be summoned regularly, but summoned as wanted by the President, according to the nature of the matters to be submitted to the Committee. When summoned they will of course form part of the Committee. It will also probably be often necessary for the Committee to require the presence of other persons who are not Privy Councillors, but they will only attend to give information, without taking part in the deliberations of the Committee. . . .

Cab. 37/40/64

2 Committee of Defence

Memorandum by the Duke of Devonshire[2]

The changes which are about to take place in the Admiralty and War Office seem to make the present a convenient time for considering whether the Defence Committee of the Cabinet is to be continued, and, if so, whether any change in its composition or procedure should be made.

The Committee has not been, I think, altogether without its use, but it has been nothing more than an informal Committee of the Cabinet, occasionally calling into Council the Commander-in-chief, the First Naval Lord, or other professional advisers, and it certainly has not occupied that place in naval and military administration which the Royal Commission, of which I was Chairman, had in view, or which, I think, was intended when it was instituted at the beginning of the present Government.

The Committee has met rarely, and generally without any definite agenda. The professional members have generally only been present during a part of the proceedings, and have rather been asked to give information on certain points, or to explain certain plans or proposals, than to take part in discussions.

No Minutes have been kept, and in general there have been no definite decisions to record. Either there has been a general understanding and agreement which the Department concerned had afterwards to embody in a complete form, or else conflicting opinions have been expressed on which the Committee had no authority to decide, and which had to be remitted for further inter-Departmental discussion or Cabinet decision.

This Committee, as I have said, has not, I think, been altogether useless, and has perhaps relieved the Cabinet from some professional

[2] Lord President of the Council.

discussions; but it has not been what the public and Parliament understood by a Committee of Defence, and if no attempt is to be made to constitute it on a more regular basis, I think that the name had better be abandoned.

If, on the other hand, it is considered that the Committee might be developed into a more useful institution, I should be prepared to propose certain changes in its procedure of which the principal would be that it should meet at certain definite intervals, that it should have a Secretary or Joint Secretaries, and that agenda for its meetings should be prepared, as well as Minutes of its proceedings kept; but it would, in the first place, be of great advantage if the present First Lord and Secretary of State for War would give their opinions for the consideration of their successors.

D.

November 2, 1900

Memorandum by Lord Lansdowne[3]
. . . In my view it is necessary, considering the great size of the Cabinet, that there should be a Committee of this sort. . . .

Cab. 37/53/71

3   The Constitution of the Defence Committee

A note by the Prime Minister, 29 February 1904
The Defence Committee was reconstituted on a new basis in December 1902. Since then it has sat frequently, and done much valuable work. We have, therefore, some experience of what, as at present constituted, it is able to perform, and some guide as the modifications and developments of which it may be capable of in the future [*sic*].

In considering its constitutional position, it is necessary to observe that in one fundamental particular it differs from any other part of our existing governmental machinery. It is *consultative*, not *executive*. It has no administrative functions: it cannot prescribe a policy to the Cabinet, nor give directions to the Army or to the Navy. Its duty is purely to advise; and though advice on military matters in which the Prime Minister, the Secretary of State for War, the First Lord of the Admiralty, and their technical assistants are agreed, is advice almost certain to be taken, still, the Defence Committee, *as such*, has no power to enforce it.

This limitation is important from more than one point of view.

[3] Secretary of State for Foreign Affairs.

In the first place, the Committee thus constituted interferes with no existing authority. In the second place, it is unnecessary to confer upon it statutory powers—a great advantage when we remember how unadaptable machinery created by Act of Parliament is apt to be. No fixed constitution for the Committee need be framed; the persons composing it need not be formally enumerated, nor is any elaborate definition of their duties and powers required. As a consequence of the flexibility thus obtained, it becomes far easier (as I shall presently show) to make the Committee a truly Imperial body, in which the Colonies as well as the mother country may find an appropriate machinery for dealing in common with the greatest of their common interests—the interests of Imperial Defence.

In order to gain the full advantage which this flexibility of constitution is able to confer, it seems undesirable to assume that the Committee should contain any *ex officio* Members at all—except, indeed, the Prime Minister for the time being. At first sight this appears open to the objection that, while the opinions of the Committee ought to command weight with the Government and Parliament, the actual decisions taken in the name of that body might really be due to a single individual —namely, the Prime Minister himself. But this peril—in any case more theoretical than real—is wholly obviated by the fact that Minutes of every meeting are preserved, and that the names of the persons present are recorded. In estimating the authority, therefore, which should attach to any decision, account can always be taken of the persons by whom it is recommended, as well as of the arguments adduced in its support. . . .

. . . To sum up: The Defence Committee, as I conceive it, would be an advisory body summoned by the Prime Minister of the day to aid him in the consideration of the wider problems of Imperial Defence. A permanent staff would be provided to give it assistance and continuity. Only the persons summoned would have the right to attend. In the vast majority of cases, perhaps in all, the Navy and the Army would be represented by their Parliamentary heads and by their expert advisers. Other persons would be summoned as the particular occasion required. But nothing in the constitution of the Committee would fetter the Prime Minister's discretion in the choice of its Members. He would be compelled neither to add unnecessarily to its numbers, nor to exclude from its deliberations persons specially qualified to assist them.

At each meeting all Members would be on an equality. Though in practice some of them would be summoned almost as of course, yet they would be there because they *were* summoned, and not as of right. There would, therefore, be no distinction of dignity between one Member and another; the Committee would be small enough to be effective; and its constitution would vary with the varying problems it was required to consider. This flexibility would be impossible if the Committee had a statutory right to give orders or determine policy; it is only attainable so long as the Committee restricts itself to advice.

The value of this advice will depend, of course, upon the reasonings by which it is supported, and upon the authority of the persons giving it. A permament record of both will be kept in the archives of the Department, and will be communicated to the Sovereign.

If a Colony desires to discuss its position in the general scheme of Imperial Defence, its Delegate would, of course, be asked to join the Committee. He would attend its deliberations so long as the questions in which his Government had a direct interest were under discussion: and he would attend as a full Member. The value of such consultations in producing co-operation between the different parts of the Empire, is, I believe, beyond our present power of estimation. And they would have no drawbacks. They could not excite jealousy or suspicion. They would interfere with no rights of self-government: and the advice in which they issued, though it might guide, could never coerce either the Colonies or the Mother Country. And here we have a further reason, if a further reason be required, for refusing to confer on the Committee executive powers. The Colonies would certainly object to handing over to any Committee, howsoever constituted, the right to impose on them a policy, to which, for financial or other reasons, they might, on consideration, feel a strong objection: and I think the Colonies would be right.

A. J. B.[4]

29th February, 1904

Cab. 37/69/33

4 Army Reform and the military needs of the Empire

A note by the Prime Minister, 22 June 1904

[This Note has been discussed and approved by the Committee of Defence.]

[4] The Prime Minister, A. J. Balfour.

In framing any scheme for reorganizing the army we have to consider—

1. The military needs of the Empire;
2. The financial position of Great Britain;
3. The sentiments of the country and of the army, to which any scheme involving large reductions of existing units will do inevitable violence. . . .

. . . Our conclusions on all these points can only be approximate. . . .

For purposes of discussion I make the following tentative observations on the first of the considerations referred to above, namely, the purposes for which the British army exists, and the forces necessary to carry those purposes into effect:

(a) The ordinary Indian garrison, say 74,400 men of all arms; and

(b) the Colonial garrisons (including for the present 20,000 men in South Africa), say 50,400 men, must be maintained.

(c) The home arsenals and protected ports must be garrisoned, and garrisoned in time to prevent a surprise at or before the declaration of war.

No questions of much difficulty seem to arise in connection with any of these statements, though we must now finally make up our minds whether Bermuda, Halifax, and Esquimault are to be garrisoned by British troops as heretofore or not.

(d) Reinforcements for India in case of war with Russia must be provided. . . .

A. J. B.

22nd June, 1904

Cab. 37/71/84

5 Officers and men defending naval and commercial harbours in the colonies and dependencies, 17 December 1904

COLONIES AND DEPENDENCIES

	Officers	Men	Total	Regulars Officers	Regulars Men	Regulars Total	Colonials Officers	Colonials Men	Colonials Total	Native Officers	Native Men	Native Total
Cape	190	4,406	4,596	129	2,406	2,535	61	2,000	2,061			
Bermuda	143	3,597	3,740	120	2,886	3,006	23 Auxiliaries	711	734			
Ceylon	178	3,795	3,973	83	1,487	1,570	91	2,061	2,152	4	247	251
Esquimalt	64	1,008	1,072	16	348	364	48	660	708			
Gibraltar	225	5,290	5,515	225	5,290	5,515						
Halifax	172	3,264	3,436	73	1,726	1,799	99	1,538	1,637			
Hong Kong	205	4,878	5,083	128	1,452	1,580	21	218	239	56	3,208	3,264
Jamaica	103	2,166	2,269	77	748	825	26	577	603		841	841
Malta	458	12,437	12,895	404	10,257	10,661	54 Militia	2,180	2,234			
Mauritius	129	3,474	3,603	93	1,484	1,577				36	1,990	2,026
St. Helena	24	611	635	20	511	531	4	100	104			
St. Lucia	75	1,572	1,647	75	915	990					657	657
Singapore	136	3,449	3,585	83	1,482	1,565	33	783	816	20	1,184	1,204
Wei-hai Wei	18	537	555	18	15	33					522	522
Sierra Leone	134	3,062	3,196	118	256	374	16	498	514		2,308	2,308
Grand total, Colonies and Dependencies	2,254	53,546	55,800	1,662	31,263	32,925	476	11,327	11,802	116	10,957	11,073

17 December 1904

Foreign Office S. (Selborne)

Cab. 37/73/165

V

DISCUSSION OF BRITISH IMPERIAL POLICY

These documents supplement those in the first part of the book mainly concerned with conferences. The first two represent consideration of British Imperial policy by Cabinet ministers and the parliamentary under-secretary. Subsequent extracts contain statements of British government intentions to non-self-governing territories, with the exception of that of J. H. Thomas.

1 Lord Selborne on Crown Colony government

Minute by Lord Selborne, 3 August 1895

. . . I summarise my view of the change demanded from two points of view, one internal and the other external to Trinidad itself. If the government of the island were that of a Crown colony pure and simple, I should advise against this proposal on these grounds. Given the principle of elected members there are only two alternatives. Either the franchise must be based upon high fancy property qualification with a still higher qualification for candidates, in which case we should establish not popular government but an oligarchy; or the change must be made on a genuinely democratic basis, in which case we should hand over the government of the island to a population fitted for such a responsibility neither by education nor by political training nor by race. But, as Mr. Wingfield points out, the unofficial members have already a majority, and thro' their finance committee they have obtained financial control. I agree with him that the regime he proposes to substitute framed on his lines would be an improvement on the present one, and regarding the matter from the point of view of Trinidad itself I should be prepared to recommend that the changes he proposes should be made, if, but only if, those who know the West Indies well can give good reasons for believing (if they do believe) that such a concession by the Secretary of State would not be merely used as the starting point for a fresh and eventually probably successful agitation having for its object to get rid of these very advantages for the sake of which alone the Secreetary of State had made the consession. (N.B.? *do the constitutions of Jamaica and Mauritius work well.*) But I feel that the question must also be considered from a wider point of view, a point of view external to Trinidad itself, the point of view in fact of the Empire at large.

I am much struck by the ever recurring argument in these papers 'Jamaica and Mauritius have had the principle conceded to them, why not Trinidad?' I am told (I naturally have no knowledge yet myself on the subject) that the mutterings of a similar agitation have already been heard from Hong Kong and Ceylon. If this is true, then I am bound to ask whether, if this demand is granted, we shall not be confronted with the argument in its turn of 'Trinidad has had the principle conceded to it, why not Hong Kong and Ceylon?' I need not dilate on the very grave objections to any divergence from the pure Crown Colony principle in the case of Hong Kong, a vast depôt of trade, a great naval station and a fortress, now more than ever to be regarded from the naval military point of view since the emergence of Japan into the position of a great naval power, nor in the case of ... Ceylon, which must be considered in exactly the same category as India. But I must ask those, who have the knowledge and experience, to say whether or no any concession in the case of Trinidad would in their opinion act as a stimulus to similar movements in Hong Kong and Ceylon and render more difficult the task of the Secretaty of State in refusing such demands. Unless, therefore, any questions about Trinidad itself and about the other great crown colonies can be satis-factorily answered, I do not think that the change now demanded in the constitution of Trinidad should be allowed to take place.

S.[1]3/8/95
C.O. 295/363

2 The Suez Canal Shares Scheme

(a) *Memorandum by the Secretary of State for the Colonies, 15 November 1895*

... Up to the present time the Imperial Government have done hardly anything to aid our Colonies and dependencies in opening up the countries which are under the British flag. We have trusted entirely

[1] Lord Selborne, Parliamentary Under-Secretary of State for the Colonies.

to individual enterprise and private capital; and while it is a subject of just pride that these have worked wonders, and have produced results not equalled by those foresign countries which have given large contributions to their colonial possessions, yet it is certain that in many cases progress has been delayed, and in some cases absolutely stayed, because the only methods by which improvement could be carried out were beyond the scope of private resources.

12. As an instance, the recent case of East Africa may be quoted. It is clear that many years, and perhaps generations, would have elapsed before the Uganda Railway would have been constructed by any private Corporation; yet without the railway no progress would be possible, and the vast territory recently acquired by the United Kingdom would remain an 'undeveloped estate' for an indefinite period of time.

13. The same state of things exists in some of our older Colonies. In Dominica, in British Honduras, and in British Guiana, for instance, there are untold possibilities of natural wealth in the shape of gold and other minerals, dye-woods and timber, and all tropical productions, which neither the Colonies themselves nor individual adventurers are in a position to open up. Crown estates of immense extent and undoubted intrinsic value are waiting a purchaser, because there are no proper means of access. Individual enterprise will till the fields, and cut the timber, and work the mines; but Government, and Government alone, can make the roads and the railways. This is the true province of Government in new countries, and until it is recognized by Great Britain she will not have fulfilled her obligations to the dependencies which she holds under her rule.

14. A policy of this kind need not entail cost to the taxpayers of this country. It ought to be made self-supporting, and even profitable, while the indirect advantage in the extension of opportunities for trade are incalculable. What the Government must do is to advance capital, to wait a reasonable time for any return, and to take some risk in each individual case, although on the average the risk will be reduced to nothing.

15. But, in order that a new policy of this kind should be successful, there must be some sort of continuity in it. It ought not to be subject to the fluctuations of the ordinary revenue—to be encouraged when there is a surplus, and sternly discountenanced when there is a deficit. Wherever and whenever a case can be made out for an investment in public works in our Colonies, which gives a satisfactory promise of a fair commercial return after a reasonable time, it ought to be considered

on its merits, and without regard to the temporary exigencies of domestic finance.

16. The falling in of the Suez Canal shares offers an opportunity of securing such a continuity of policy, and would provide a fund from which these investments might be made, without calling on the British taxpayer to find a penny, even in the extreme event of every investment proving to be an utter loss. . . .

. . . 19. I believe that such a policy would be very popular in the country, since it would give an immediate impetus to trade by the expenditure which would be made on the various works sanctioned, while it would permanently increase the commerce of the Empire by opening up new fields for private enterprise and new markets for British industry.

J. Chamberlain.[2]

Colonial Office,
  November 15, 1895.

(b) *Memorandum by the Chancellor of the Exchequer, 8 January 1896*[3]

. . . I cannot agree in Mr. Chamberlain's opinion that 'up to the present time the Imperial Government have done hardly anything to aid our Colonies and dependencies in opening up the countries which are under the British flag'. The case of East Africa, which he quotes, is an instance to the contrary: Parliament has readily undertaken large expenditure there, of all kinds, in opening up the country. And this is really but a continuation of a long settled policy. I suppose that no new Colony has been started without large grants-in-aid: Fiji is the latest example. And these grants-in-aid have in some cases been repeatedly made, as on the West Coast of Africa. Nor do I know with what other object we have spent millions in South African wars, except the protection and development of the Cape and Natal. No doubt there have been times when the grant of Imperial aid for these objects was much less popular than it has been of late years. But the fact that it is almost universally popular now is rather an argument against the necessity of an alteration in the system by which it is given. At present there is no reason for attempting to conceal charges of this kind from the public or removing them in any degree from the control of Parliament. They are cheerfully voted, and a Government gains credit by incurring them. . . .

Cab. 37/41/1

---

[2] Secretary of State for the Colonies.   [3] Sir M. Hicks-Beach.

3   Harcourt on the Crown Colonies and protectorates

House of Commons Speech, 27 June 1912

Mr. L. Harcourt:[4] . . . the changes . . . in the six years [of the existence of the present Government] in representative Government and administration in the Crown Colonies and Protectorates. Legislative Councils with unofficial, as well as official members, have been established in Nyasaland and the East African Protectorate. In Ceylon the constitution has been remodelled by the substitution of the principle of election for that of nomination, so far as was considered possible, for the Legislative Council . . . In the Malay Peninsula, in 1909, Siam transferred to the British Crown her Protectorate over Kedah, Perlis, Trengganu and Kalantan . . . and . . . an important step was taken in the consolidation of the Federated Malay States by the creation of a Federal Council, consisting of the High Commissioner and the native rulers, with the Chief Secretary and British Residents, and a number of unofficial members to legislate for the whole Federation. In the West Indies, in 1909, there was a lowering of the franchise in British Guiana. In Basutoland a National Council was finally established by Proclamation in 1910 . . . the Nigerias, where by far the greatest change in administration is in process of gestation. . . .

Hansard 5s., 1912, 40, 511

4   Amery on reconstruction in the dependent Empire

House of Commons Speech, 30 July 1919

Lieut.-Colonel Amery:[5] . . . East Africa . . . was the first community in the British Empire to impose conscription. More than two-thirds of the male inhabitants in that colony took the field. The white population of Rhodesia showed a similarly patriotic ardour. As regards native troops . . . The West African forces, the King's African Rifles, and the West Indies Regiment, between them put something like 80,000 combatant troops into the field, and very much more than

[4] Secretary of State for the Colonies.
[5] Parliamentary Under-Secretary of State for the Colonies.

half a million carriers and other auxiliaries were raised in the African Colonies to carry on the campaign in Africa and in other regions of the world. . . . The Colonies themselves have in every instance contributed from their revenue a substantial sum towards the cost of the War. . . .

. . . Reconstruction in the outer Empire, just as much as here at home, must mean something more than the restoration of pre-war conditions. It must mean that we must set up a new and more positive standard of our duty and obligation towards the peoples to whom this House is in the position of a trustee and to those territories whose boundless potentialities call urgently for development in the interests of their own inhabitants, of the British Empire as a whole, and of the impoverished and wasted world . . .

. . . An additional reason for setting a new standard in our task of reconstruction is that by the terms of the Treaty of Peace large territories will be assigned to us under a mandate. I do not think that that mandate is likely to impose upon us any conditions which we would not impose on ourselves or which we have not been in the habit of imposing upon ourselves whenever we dealt with subject peoples. We have always in very large measures treated native territories under our rule as a mandate to us in the interests of the inhabitants and of the world at large, and we have justified our authority not merely in our own interests, but by the general consent of other nations with regard to our rule. . . .

. . . the ideal towards which we are aiming in the sphere for which the Colonial Office is responsible is the same ideal which is found throughout the rest of our Dominions, the ideal of self-government, the participation of the people of the country, in so far as they are capable of it, in the government of the country. The difficulties of advancing in that direction are very great. In some cases these difficulties arise owing to the backward condition of the population, whom it would be a crime to allow to walk unassisted at the present time. In other cases, where the population is of the smallest and most scattered character you cannot decide that a community with a population equal to a second or third-class city in this country has all the attributes of self-government, even though in other respects it might be fit for it. Again you may have a case, as in Gibraltar or Malta, where the population live within the precincts of a military fortress or live immediately around a great military or naval fortress. All these things do make the problem difficult and complex. Critics in this House may say sometimes that we are slow in making progress, that we see the difficulties rather more clearly than they do, or that those difficulties seem more serious to us. But I would like to give them this assurance that, though we are not able to move as rapidly as they would wish us in some respects, at any rate we have the same ultimate goal in mind as they have.

. . . It is not enough for the Government merely to try to hold an even balance between the desire of the planter to get plenty of cheap workmen and their duty towards seeing that the native is well treated and remunerated. More than that, we want to see that production is not hampered by the absence of willing and understanding, wishful workers in this field. Our main hope, at least a very large avenue of development, lies in inducing the native to become his own employer, his own cultivator—to make him realise the advantage and the profit of becoming an intelligent cultivator. That has been done with very considerable success in many parts of the world. In the Gold Coast, for instance, we have induced the natives to take up with great enthusiasm 'on their own,' not as workers in the plantations, the cultivation of cocoa, and the output of cocoa from the Gold Coast has gone up from 960 tons in 1901 to 120,000 tons now—about half the whole world's production of cocoa. The cultivation of cotton in Uganda, and of sugar in many of the West Indies, has developed very appreciably by what has been called the small farmer development, by getting the native himself to grow for profit. . . .

. . . There is a very large task before us, both in general education and, perhaps more particularly, in practical education in agriculture. We want to strengthen all our Agricultural Departments. We want to start, for study and research, agricultural colleges, or universities, if you like, which will be the centres from which new ideas and better methods will be diffused to all the surrounding Colonies . . . we have been fortunate in securing from the Treasury a Grant of £20,000 a year for special research work in those Colonies which are not able to do research work themselves, on the lines on which very much larger sums have been granted for research work in this country.

. . . we have been too timid in capitalising the territories under our charge, and I think that certainly, as compared with the Dominions, the Crown Colonies and Protectorates are under-capitalised. I should like to give some figures which certainly convey that impression. I saw some figures the other day—they are not official; they are from the 'Financier'—about the general investments in the Dominions and the Colonies. Up to 1914, all investments in this country of all kinds in the Dominions amounted to something like £1,300,000,000, and the sum total of the investments in the Crown Colonies and Protectorates was £120,000,000, or less than a tenth of the investments in the Dominions. The amount of public loans raised in the Dominions is about £320,000,000, and in that I am not counting the loans raised during the War, while in the Crown Colonies and Protectorates the total is £22,000,000. I think, there again, there is on the face of it reasonable argument for thinking that we ought to invest more capital in the development of the Crown Colonies and Protectorates. . . . The prime object, of course, of that development must be the welfare of the inhabitants of those regions. Our first duty is to them; our object is not to exploit them, but to enable them materially, as well as in every other respect, to rise to a higher plane of living and civilisation. But . . . we cannot develop them and help them without an over-spill of wealth and prosperity that would be an immense help to this country in the difficult times that lie ahead. . . .

I should like also to say a word about the constitutional development in the relations between ourselves and the great self-governing Dominions, because that has been one of the most remarkable features in the development of the British Constitution during the last two years. We went into this War without having the time and without having the machinery through which we could take the opinion of the Empire as a whole on our policy. We had to act on our own decision, and happily the whole of the Empire endorsed that decision. But it was obvious that was not satisfactory, and a clear pledge was given by Mr. Asquith's Government that in the settlement of the terms of Peace the Dominions would have the fullest opportunity, not only of considering, but have a voice in deciding. During the last two years, by the happy device of what came to be known as the Imperial Cabinet, we have had a machinery both for consultation and for decisions. I was privileged to act as the Secretary of that body during its sessions, and whatever may be said about the novelty of the peculiar constitutional form of a Cabinet which as far as execution goes has to act through a number of autonomous and separate bodies, the fact still remains that the common policy of the Empire, as regards the conduct of war, as regards the ever-pressing foreign questions that arose while the Imperial Cabinet was in session, as regards considering and laying down what we wished the terms of peace to be, was carried out as a single policy by a body of men who gained a single view of these matters and worked together as effectively as a Cabinet can work.

That process has been carried on at the Conference in Paris, and it has had two sides. The one that has most impressed the outside world is the fact that at that Conference the full equality of the Dominions with ourselves as nations has been recognised, not only by us, but by the other Governments. They have been treated not only as equal nations within the brotherhood of the British Empire, but as equal nations with other nations outside the Empire, and I know that there are some timid Imperialists, I might perhaps call them, who are rather startled by this, who think it is a beginning of the end of any effective Imperial unity. My conviction is exactly the contrary. I have always been convinced that closer Imperial unity could only be based on the recognition of the fullest equality of status between ourselves and the other Dominions of the Empire, and that conviction has only been strengthened by what has happened in the last few months, because while on the one hand that Conference has recognised equality in the national status of the Dominions, that Conference has seen the Dominions and ourselves working together on the British Empire Delegation, which for the time being took the place of the Imperial Cabinet, as a single body with one mind, one thought, and one policy. The policy which the Prime Minister of this country brought back from the Peace Conference was not the United Kingdom policy, but the policy hammered out by the whole Empire, and on every Committee of that Conference the Dominions were represented, not as representing the Dominions, but as representing the British Empire. It was as representing the British Empire that Mr. Hughes was chairman of the Commission on indemnities, and it was as representing the British Empire that Sir Robert Borden dealt with the problem of territorial delimitation in the Near East. The more the principle of equality is openly established to the world, the greater the effective unity of the British Empire. How that unity is to take a constitutional shape in the future no one can say. It has been agreed at the Conference of 1917 that as soon as may be after the conclusion of Peace a special constitutional conference is to assemble and to consider how, on the basis of those principles of autonomy and equality, effective common action can be taken in foreign policy and all cognate matters. I do not know whether that conference will be able to come to any definite conclusion, or what it may recommend. The difficulties in the way of any solution are enormous, but I do say this, that, difficult as the problem may be, it cannot be impossible, because no man has a right to call that impossible which for the last six months has been a reality in practice. The Empire has existed in fact and in practice as a unity for working purposes, and to my mind it is inconceivable that such a unity cannot . . . be in some shape or form attained in the future.

Hansard 5s., 118, 2172–86

5 Amery on colonial affairs

House of Commons Speech, 11 August 1920
Lieut.-Colonel Amery: . . . I have been in parts of the Empire where I have met the settler and the pioneer . . . I have no less had opportunities of meeting the natives, and I have come back . . . fully conscious . . . of the greatness of the task that lies upon this country in lifting up and helping forward the native population for which we are trustees. . . . I wish to assert . . . that our goal in the administration of the Dependencies of the Empire is the same as the goal of any Department of this country, the same as the goal that the India Office sets before itself, namely, to enable every part of the Empire to obtain, in the fullness of time, and when conditions make it possible, full power of controlling its own affairs and developing its own destinies. . . .

. . . But we have to consider all the difficulties of each problem in its own setting . . . in . . . one case in the last year we have proceeded from a Colonial Office administration where the majority was official, and the elected members were in a pure minority, to a very wide measure of responsible government.

. . . In Malta we are giving to a population not of British birth, in respect of all the more important functions of Government, full responsible Government by Ministers elected by themselves.

. . . We are responsible . . . not only for moving towards freer Government in the Colonies, but we are in the meantime also responsible for peace, order and good Government, and we are responsible for the interest of every class of the community. It by no means follows that the immediate grant of full responsible Government in communities of that character would be consistent either with peace or with the welfare of the mass of the people. . . . to give complete self-Government straight away to communities like Rhodesia or the East African Protectorate, on any sort of franchise, would not be in the interests of the mass of the native population, and I believe the same could be said if you here and now put the whole power of Government in a country like Ceylon into that small handful of lawyers who in the main would get the power.

. . . In local matters we are in this present year giving Ceylon a

Local Government Ordinance under which urban and district councils can be set up which will contain an elected majority and an elected chairman. . . .

. . . where you have countries that are organised right through on the community basis, and where communities represent not only different races and religions, but different economic factors and functions, then to have a purely geographical territorial representation would simply mean that the minority communities would absolutely disappear politically and secure no representation whatever of their interests and of their views. Therefore, we cannot accept that point of view. In every case where we have given these special franchises, we have done so because they have urged it upon us. But the communal franchises are not necessarily permanent. When they have served their purpose, possibly proportional representation, or something else which may secure the same object, may enable us to do away with them.

Hansard 5s., 133, 490-94

6 J. H. Thomas on Dominion affairs

House of Commons Speech, 18 April 1929
   Mr. J. H. Thomas:[6] . . . I have never hesitated to say—and I always endeavour to act up to that in practice—that although there may be, indeed there must inevitably be, party differences on question of policy, that so far as the unity, the development and the prosperity of the Empire are concerned, there is no real essential difference between any parties in the House.

Hansard 5s., 227, 434

7 Amery on colonial policy

House of Commons Speech, 30 April 1929
   Mr. Amery:[7] . . . During the last five years 20 members of the staff of the Colonial Office, including my right hon. Friend and myself, have been on one or more visits of varying duration to Colonies or groups of Colonies, and some 27 members of the various Colonial Services have worked shorter or longer periods in the Office itself. Further, by the system inaugurated in 1927 regular Colonial Office

---

[6] Member for Derby.   [7] Secretary of State for the Colonies.

Conferences will be held to keep the Office still more closely in association and mutual understanding with the services outside.

. . . All these developments, which affect the life of every individual
in all these communities, are bound to be reflected in the political
ideas and aspirations of the people. Quite apart from the stimulus
given by the Great War to demands for self-government or self-
determination, the whole process of development has been, from the
point of view of the lives of the people themselves, a revolutionary
one. It naturally compels us to face the question of how that revolution
is to be accommodated to the framework of government. The problem
which we had to solve in the Dominions many years ago was a comparatively simple one. We were dealing with communities which had
self-government, its methods and traditions, in their blood. Here we
are dealing with an infinitely more complex situation. We have to
deal with people very few of whom have ever had any experience
of self-government at all. We have to deal with every variety of race
and of religion, and with people at every stage of development, and,
very often, every stage of development side by side in the same community. Problems of that character are not susceptible of any simple or
any single solution. We have got to feel our way tentatively towards
the solution of these problems.

There is, indeed, one broad principle which I think has begun to
emerge in recent years, and that is that any development based on the
idea of representative, as against responsible government, namely,
based on the confrontation of an irremovable executive with an elected
majority, with no responsibility for the conduct of government, leads
either to paralysis or to continuous friction and trouble. Therefore,
what we want to aim at, where time is given us, is the endeavour to
build up a tradition of responsibility from the beginning, and wherever
we can find the nucleus of any existing machinery or tradition on which
the sense of responsible self-government can be built up, to make the
fullest use of that. It was that principle which inspired the whole
system of indirect government in Northern Nigeria, a conception
which has since spread widely to other parts of the Empire and which
has been largely reproduced, where conditions permitted it, in Southern
Nigeria. In the Gold Coast it has been linked up with the Central
Legislature of the colony by the very interesting experiment of the
provincial councils of chiefs. In Tanganyika Sir Donald Cameron has
. . . reconstructed wherever he could find them the elements of real
native government and of a native sense of responsibility. In Kenya
the native councils have, with somewhat different methods, followed

the same principle. In Uganda we have something not far off a native parliament in the Lukiko. But there are many other places, where there are no such existing historical foundations to build on, or where development in other directions has advanced so far that you cannot wait for the slow process of building up. . . .

In British Guiana a curious, ancient and extraordinarily unworkable constitution, which provided neither efficient financial administration nor any real training in responsibility, which might have paved the way towards self-government in the future, has given place . . . to a system of a more normal character. . . . In Ceylon a similar difficulty was investigated by the Commission under Lord Donoughmore. That Commission has made very far-reaching and interesting proposals. Not the least interesting was the suggestion that training in responsibility should be given, short of what is ordinarily known as responsible Cabinet Government, by a system of Committees parallel to that which does the work of the League of Nations or, nearer home, the work of our great municipalities. . . .

An even more difficult problem in many respects is that of Kenya. There you have to deal with a white community which has self-government in its blood and which, if it had stood alone, would naturally expect self-government after a certain reasonable increase in its numerical strength. But it is not alone. It lives side by side with other peoples, and while we hope to associate that community with us in an increasing measure in the responsibility of trusteeship, yet it is obviously out of the question, in any time that we are dealing with at this moment, to consider handing over responsible self-government to that small body. Of course no one can set an absolute limit to the future. Progress in the future must depend upon future development. At this moment we are dealing with particular and limited problems and with regard to that I will only say that we have had the advantage of the many very valuable recommendations of the Commission presided over by . . . (Sir H. Young). The whole matter is being now or will be in the next few weeks freely discussed without any limitation or restriction by Sir Samuel Wilson with every community concerned, and will be the subject of discussion and consideration by this House in the next Parliament before any decision can be arrived at.

. . . The particular problem of the Kenya constitution is . . . only an incidental aspect of a problem of a very different character which the Hilton Young Commission went out to investigate, a problem more administrative and developmental than constitutional, namely, the degree of greater unity which may be feasible in those East African territories which were divided, not by any natural divisions, but by purely arbitrary political divisions, in the eighties of the last century, and which from the point of view of transport, development, defence and many other considerations, are essentially one more or less homogeneous territory.

. . . The problem of the closer union of adjoining colonies has also to be faced in other parts of the Empire. I would like to say a word about the satisfactory West Indian Conference which met in Barbados a little time ago. That conference was the result of a preliminary conference which I convened in London three years ago at which it was decided to set up regular conference machinery on the lines of the Imperial Conference. The result of that first conference is most encouraging to anyone who believes as I do that the destiny of the British West Indian Colonies is gradually to draw closer and closer to each other. . . .

Hansard, 5s., 227, 1421–6

8   Dr. Shiels on colonial policy

House of Commons Speech, 11 December 1929
The Under-Secretary of State for the Colonies (Dr. Drummond Shiels):
. . . this House is directly responsible for the welfare of from 50,000,000 to 70,000,000 of human beings . . . .

There are some 36 British colonies and protectorates, including the mandated territories. In the administration of those dependencies there are about 60,000 colonial public service officials engaged.

. . . The coloured peoples of the Empire present many variations of race and culture and no uniform policy is possible or desirable. There are, however, certain general principles which govern British policy and administration. . . . These general principles have been set out in various documents, but as time is short I shall not quote from any of them. Suffice it for me to say that the Government accept fully the principles of the Devonshire[8] and similar declarations in the spirit and in the letter. The method of the application of these principles is a matter which necessarily arouses controversy from time to time, but the principles themselves, I hope, are clear.

. . . I would like to say one word about education. . . . Out of roughly 15,000,000 children of school age, only 2,500,000 are enrolled as scholars, and I think one of the strongest criticisms that can be made of

8 Cmd 1922 of 1923.

our past Colonial history is for our neglect of primary education. I feel that many of our difficulties in Kenya would have been lessened to-day if the provision of primary education had been put into operation many years ago. A year ago an advisory committee on education in the Colonies was appointed. It superseded a committee on native education in Africa which existed some years previously . . . in Achimota in the West and in Makerere in the East are two great institutions which might well be the genesis of African universities. . . .

I feel that education and the encouragement of the development of self-governing institutions are the two most important requirements in our Colonial Empire policy. In this connection I am very much interested in the question of the gradual development of Legislative Councils from official and nominated to elected assemblies and with the increase, in number and importance, of local self-governing bodies as a training ground for the larger spheres. This development has been seriously neglected, and we have lost a fine recruiting ground for administrators who might have eased the situation in many directions.

. . . There is also the question of franchise and representation, about which I would have liked to have said something. There is great need also for industrial legislation. A number of Colonies have no Workmen's Compensation Act, no Employers' Liability Act, and only very primitive factory legislation, or none at all. Then there is the important question of wage regulations. These are matters which ought to be explored. . . .

Hansard 5s., 233, 611–15

9   The second Colonial Office Conference, June and July 1930

Speeches by Lord Passfield and Dr. Shiels

The Secretary of State for the Colonies Lord Passfield: . . . the great change which has come about, since I was in this office forty years ago, as regards the purpose and the object of the administration of these semi-tropical and tropical Colonies. I do not refer merely to the Mandated Territories, where the British Government has accepted the obligation of an express trusteeship for the several native populations, as peoples which are unable to stand alone in the competition of the modern world, that is to say, His Majesty's Government has accepted the obligation of directing its administration to their improvement in material and moral progress. That is not a new thing.

It has already been, I think, the basis of British administration, at any rate for half a century, but I should like to remind you that it is now emphasised and expressed and accepted by the British Government as an obligation in the Covenant of the League of Nations, not exactly in the same terms as for the Mandated Territories, but in terms equivalent. Consequently the Government of every Colony, equally with the Government of a Mandated Territory, is under an express obligation to promote the welfare and advancement in civilisation of its native population. As I say, it is not a new object in British colonial administration, but the emphatic declaration that the Government is now under an obligation to the rest of the world to see that that is done is in itself a great change. Such an advance must always be the underlying main purpose of every colonial administration, and I look to see the separate Colonies putting themselves very much on a par with the Mandated Territories in that respect. It is true they are not at present subject to review and criticism by a Permanent Mandates Commission of the League of Nations, but our obligation, the obligation of the British Government, is the same for the one as for the other. Therefore, we have to report, if not to the League of Nations at present, we have to report to the world what we are doing in that way, and, in particular, I venture to suggest to you that the report or documents of the chief native commissioner or other officer having that sort of duty must be put in the form of a report not on the native population but on the social and economic advance of the native population during the preceding year. We must be able to show to the world that there is some advance taking place, not necessarily a universal advance. . . .

The Parliamentary Under-Secretary Dr. Drummond Shiels: . . . We have, I hope, shown at these sessions and otherwise that a Labour Government is as concerned with the efficiency of machinery and with the extension of the latest achievements of science to our Colonial Empire as a Government of any shade of political opinion could be. . . . I think also that Governors will agree that since we came into office we have not issued any revolutionary edicts or urged any extreme reversal of local policy. We realize it would not be wise, even if it were possible or desired, to have the lines of policy in our overseas territories changed about in response to political changes at home. At the same time, each form of Government at home—if it is a Government interested in these matters—must give its own emphasis to aspects of policy, and the subjects we are discussing today represent some of these in which the Labour Party is particularly interested, and in connection with which its principles can be specially applied. In

'Labour and the Nation' and in the paper on 'Native Labour in East Africa' recently issued, we have set out our views on the principles which we believe should govern our dealings with native peoples. We believe, not only in the principles of trusteeship as admirably set forth in the Devonshire Memorandum[9] and other papers by various Governments, but also in the training of these subject peoples to develop to their fullest capacity in all directions and particularly in the direction of ultimate self-government. Whatever differences of opinion there may be as to the relative capacities of the various subject peoples of the Empire, we wish them to have every opportunity to develop to their fullest capacity, and that the process should be a steady and expanding one. . . .

I am not . . . a particular enthusiast for indirect rule, except as a stage in development. There is sometimes a tendency to regard it as the end of our Colonial policy, but, to my mind, it is by no means a perfect system of government. It is quite natural and wise to use the local and native machinery when one proceeds to administer a new country. It should, however, I feel, as far as possible be developed in a democratic direction and as many as possible of our democratic methods should be grafted on to it, particularly in the way of the ultimate election of all agents of Government. . .

C.O. 854/173

9 Cmd 1922 of 1923.

VI

THE WEST INDIES
Economic difficulties and political problems

Competition from bounty-fed beet sugar brought great difficulties for West Indian sugar in the 1880s and 1890s, and led to the despatch of a commission in 1897. Adoption of the Brussels convention in 1902 resulted in the abolition of bounties on beet sugar. Marketing problems however continued. Constitutional change in the British West Indies in the later nineteenth century ended in the restoration of a majority of official members to the Jamaica legislature in 1899. The British Government began to concede limited constitutional advance in the 1920s after the report of the Parliamentary Under-Secretary for the Colonies, Mr. Wood, in 1922. He advised against responsible government or federation.

1 The Colonial Office on government

(a) *Memorandum by C. P. Lucas, October 1897*
   . . . I think:
   1. That where Imperial money is given there should be Imperial control. In other words there should be Crown Colonies; and to payment of loans and annual subsidies should be attached, as an indispensable condition, abolition, as far as possible, of the elective element and of unofficial majorities except in purely municipal matters. There is one exception, I would not interfere with the Barbados Constitution. It goes too far back and has too much of a history. Moreover it is not proposed to give Barbados annual subsidies, but to lend it unconditionally £120,000 for the establishment of central factories, the Colonial Government being 'held responsible to the Imperial Government for both principal and interest' . . . .

C. P. L. (Lucas)[1]
October, 1897
C.O. 884/5

[1] Assistant Under-Secretary of State.

(b) *Case against the West Indian Constitutions, c. March 1898*

[This memorandum was not dated. It was probably written in the spring of 1898.]

. . . The case should be based on the following more general grounds:

1. First and foremost, it is reasonable that substantial imperial grants should be accompanied by imperial control of revenue and expenditure.

2. Representative Assemblies without responsible government, are hardly defensible in principle.

3. As a matter of fact, elsewhere they have worked badly and their main or only defence is, as was the case in the Cape that they are preliminary to complete self government.

There is no such defence in the case of the West Indies, for no one suggests that these Colonies are suited for complete self government.

4. As has been abundantly proved in English colonial history, representative institutions without responsible government lead to

(a) conflict between the executive and the legislature, and

(b) between the Colony and the Mother country.

5. If these evils have not come to light much in the case of the West Indies it is because it has been recognised that in spite of the forms, the power virtually rests at home and must rest there; but it is undeniable that the present system constantly leads to delays, needless correspondence, and some measure of bad feeling. Every time the question of the renewal of the civil list comes up in British Guiana there is a risk of a miniature constitutional crisis, such as we read of in past days in the case of Canada and other Colonies.

6. The electorates in these colonies or at any rate in some of them, are absurdly small; the constitutions are really oligarchies.

7. The West Indies have suffered from the want of capable governors and other officers; and the existence of representative Assemblies gives a standing excuse for weak governors while it tends to hamper strong ones.

8. Of all races, the negro race probably benefits most by a strong executive. Nothing weakens the executive so much as an independent legislature.

9. The present condition is quite anomalous; out of colonies, which are similar in conditions, some are Crown Colonies, some are not, and one, Jamaica, was first a representative colony, then a crown colony and now again, in a sense, a representative colony.

10. The constitutional history of these colonies is as follows, they were in great measure settled colonies and had English institutions planted in them from the first. At first the number of English settlers

in proportion to the whole population was very far larger than subsequently. As years went on through the operation of the slave system they became more and more negro colonies, and in the present century, such colonists as have come in, have been mainly coloured colonists, viz. East Indians. Thus beginning with conditions, under which self governing institutions were suitable, they have kept those institutions into times, and under conditions when they are unsuitable.

11. A very practical objection to these mixed legislatures is that they are inclined not to vote enough money for defence purposes. This has been especially the case in Mauritius which has a similar kind of constitution to that of the West Indies. . . .

C.O. 318/293

2   The condition of the West Indian colonies

Memorandum by J. Chamberlain, 8 November 1897

The Report of the West Indian Commission discloses a state of things which even now is alarming, and which in a very short time is almost certain to become disastrous and dangerous.

The prosperity of the West Indies may be said to depend entirely upon sugar. Even at the present time, after great efforts have been made to introduce other cultivation, sugar-cane products account for 53 per cent. of all the exports of all these Colonies; and, if we exclude from the calculation the exports of Jamaica, where other industries have been largely prosecuted, and also omit the gold industry of British Guiana, the proportion averages 75 per cent., and varies from *nil* in Grenada, where sugar has been abandoned, and 15 per cent. in Dominica, to 94½ per cent. in Antigua, 96½ per cent. in St. Kitts, and 97 per cent. in Barbados.

During the last fifteen years the conditions of sugar cultivation have become more and more difficult, and the industry is now in imminent risk of extinction. The consequences will not only be fatal to the sugar planters, but they will be productive of the most serious embarrassment to the local Governments. Some of the islands are already practically insolvent, and others are certain to become so. Large additional expenditure will be required to avert distress and to secure employment for the population which will be thrown out of work. It is to be feared that serious disturbances may occur if the negro population are suddenly deprived of their present means of livelihood; while large sums will be required in order to repatriate the coolies who have been imported under agreements to return them free of expense to India at the expiry of their terms of engagement.

The primary cause of this state of things is the low price of sugar . . .

It does not appear from the Report of the Commission that the state of the industry is due to bad management on the part of the planters, or to absenteeism, or to any other cause for which they themselves are primarily responsible. . . .

The Royal Commission unanimously report that the abolition of the bounty system is an object at which the Government should aim, and that the accomplishment of such an end is worth some sacrifice, provided always that such sacrifice would be really effective and would not involve evils out of proportion to those which it is desired to remove; but after the experience of the negotiations in 1887 and 1888, it is clear, and the Commissioners themselves recognize the fact, that no success could be expected from further negotiations unless the Government is prepared to legislate adversely against sugar coming from those countries which refuse to abolish bounties. . . .

. . . The Commissioners proceed to consider at some length the question of countervailing duties. Upon this point they differ in opinion, and while Sir Edward Grey and Sir David Barbour reject the proposal, Sir Henry Norman has presented a separate Report urging its acceptance. . . .

Having negatived by a majority the idea of countervailing duties, the Commissioners unanimously make certain positive recommendations, the most important of which come under the heads of:

1. Greater economy of administration.
2. Imperial subsidies.

As regards economies, very little is to be expected. They can only be effected in the number or the salaries of the officials, or in the expenditure on public works. But, having in view the probability of great distress and the increased responsibility thereby thrown on the local authorities, it would be hazardous to lower in any considerable degree the number or the class of the public servants; while a reduction in the expenditure on public works would be fatal to any hope of substituting other industries for sugar, or of providing, in the meantime, for the necessities of the population.

It is probable, on the contrary, that much larger expenditure must be immediately incurred to open up communications with Crown lands, and to arrange for the settlement upon them of the labour population and for their education in agricultural pursuits. . . .

The Commissioners recommend the gradual settlement of the

labourers as peasant proprietors, the technical education of the people in agricultural industries, the improvement both of internal and external means of communication, and the establishment of central factories for the treatment of the cane. . . .

In my opinion the Commissioners have, as is usual in these cases, altogether underestimated the cost of carrying out these proposals in an effective way. If anything is to be done to produce an early and appreciable result, and to tide the West Indies over the crisis with which they are threatened in the event of the total failure of the sugar industry, I believe that the annual demand on the people of the United Kingdom will have to be counted in hundreds of thousands of pounds.

Unfortunately there is no certainty that expenditure, even on such a scale as this, and still less if confined to the amounts mentioned in the Report, will avert a crisis or replace the West Indies in a position of prosperity or even of stability. Many years must elapse, after the failure of sugar, before the population of the Colonies now dependent on it can earn their own living or maintain civilized government without assistance.

From the above statement it will be evident that the Royal Commission have not given much assistance to the solution of the problem. They have cleared the way by demonstrating the greatness and urgency of the danger, but they have left to Her Majesty's Government the full responsibility of finding and proposing a remedy.

If the matter could be treated independently of political considerations, I should certainly recommend the renewal of negotiations for the removal of the bounties with the declared intention of placing a considerable duty on all bounty-fed sugar.

I am led to this conclusion by the following considerations:—

1. The bounty system is indefensible, and it is absolutely wrong that the United Kingdom should profit by the ruin of its oldest Colonies.

2. By taking steps to abolish them, or nullify their effect, we clear ourselves of our principal responsibility. If after this the Colonies cannot live, at least it is not our fault.

3. I do not think the arguments of the Commissioners at all conclusive as to the effect of the abolition. I believe that for a time at any rate, if not permanently, it would save the industry, and give opportunity for developing those new arrangements which all inquirers hold to be necessary. It would be a great gain if the enterprise died out gradually, instead of becoming suddenly extinct before any satisfactory preparation could be made against the inevitable consequences of such a catastrophe.

4. No alternative proposal has been, or can be, made, which offers a better hope of meeting the immediate danger or appears to involve a lesser charge to the mother country.

5. It has been strongly impressed upon me that, apart from any question of the direct and immediate effect on prices which would or might be produced by a countervailing duty, the moral and indirect result of imposing such a duty would be very considerable. It would at once, I am told, put heart into the West Indian planters; it would go far to restore the credit of their industry with their bankers and in the City; it would be taken by the colonists on the one hand, white and black alike, and by foreign competitors on the other as an intimation that the mother country intends to see fair play; and it would put an end to the grumble that the West Indies would gain more by joining the United States than by remaining British islands.

But this policy . . . will undoubtedly provoke violent opposition, and it is for the Cabinet to say if they will face it.

. . . All I need say now is that if it should be decided to take no steps with regard to the bounties, but to leave the sugar industry to its fate, it will be absolutely necessary to allocate much larger sums to the relief of the West Indian Colonies than would otherwise be the case. . . .

J. C.[2]

8 November 1897.

Cab. 37/45/44

3 Chamberlain on the situation in the West Indies

(a) *House of Commons Speech, 14 March 1898*

Mr J. Chamberlain:[3] . . . We have always had to make grants in aid of those of our Crown Colonies or Protectorates which have been unable, by themselves, to secure the necessities of ordinary administration. We undertook a responsibility with regard to these Crown Colonies and Protectorates which are distinctly under our control. We have to see that the responsibility is fulfilled, and, of course, it includes the provision of all that is necessary for reasonable and proper administration. We recognise that in the case of Protectorates which have not been developed and which are in the early stages of our possession. For instance, we take a grant at the present time for Uganda, for British Bechuanaland, for Basutoland, and we are asking, in addition, for an

[2] Joseph Chamberlain, Secretary of State for the Colonies.
[3] Secretary of State for the Colonies.

increased grant for Cyprus, and, also, we are asking for the first time this year for a grant which has been rendered necessary by the developments of other Powers in connection with our West African Colonies. . . . it is part of the necessary consequences of empire. We cannot be an Imperial Power unless we undertake to fulfil these responsibilities, but it is, no doubt, rather an exception that we should come for any grant of this kind. . . . The principle, therefore, which I ask the House to accept, is that in all cases in which we are ourselves fully responsible for the administration of the Colonies we must, if necessary, provide for the unavoidable cost of that administration, and we cannot allow these Colonies to fall into anarchy, or the necessary Services, such as education or police, to be neglected, in consequence of want of funds. But I must go a step farther. What I have said applies generally to any Crown Colony which might find itself in the position of those to which I am referring; but I do not hesitate to go farther, and say that in the case of the West Indies there is a special obligation which rests upon this country. That special obligation is referred to in the Report of the Royal Commission . . . the Royal Commissioners say that, in the case of the West Indies, the population, which is chiefly a population of negroes, has been placed in the islands by force, either by compulsion employed by this country in the old days of the slave trade, or by compulsion employed by other countries, but of which we took upon ourselves the consequences when we took possession of the Colonies; and the Commissioners go on to say—

'We have placed the labouring population where it is, and created the conditions, moral and material, under which it exists, and we cannot divert from ourselves responsibility for its future.'

I associate myself entirely with that observation, and I believe it constitutes an additional claim upon this country, in consequence of the distress which now overhangs the islands. One other remark must be made, and that is that the distress is due, as the Report of the Commissioners shows, to the failure of the sugar industry.

. . . it is the intention of the Government, in every case in which a grant is made to any of these islands, to see that we have full and absolute control over the taxation and the expenditure. I say that generally, although, perhaps, in order to be perfectly accurate, it may be necessary to make some sort of exception in the case of Barbados, which is exceptionally situated. It has a Constitution which goes back for 300 years; a Constitution which, in the case of that island, has on the whole worked well, and the economy on the whole has been fairly

satisfactory. At the present time we are not asking anything for
Barbados. . . .

Hansard, 4s., 1898, 1541-5

(b) *House of Commons Speech, 2 August 1898*

Mr. J. Chamberlain: . . . after making all the savings we can in
regard to the administration, there would still be a deficit in many of
these islands between the ordinary expenditure and the ordinary
revenue until either the sugar industry is restored to something like a
normal condition of prosperity or until some alternative industries
have been discovered which will take the place of sugar and which
will find employment for the population . . . there must be some
annual demand from this House of some grants in aid of deficits
which necessarily will accrue, and unless we are prepared to find the
money it is absolutely impossible to carry on the administration of
the islands in any proper form . . . these grants were not to be considered as doles, but as necessary to the expense of the Empire. . . .
There is nothing new in these grants. Grants of this kind have always
been made from time to time for different Colonies, and they are
absolutely inseparable from Colonial dominion. It may be thought
that Colonial dominion is, or is not, a desirable thing, and as to that I
have no doubt myself. I believe confidently that, on the whole, this
country benefits from, and it almost lives upon, its Colonial Empire.
If there is to be such a Colonial Empire we cannot allow any part of the
territory which we control and over whose finances we have complete
authority to fall into anarchy and ruin. Taking the Colonial Empire at
large, as I have said, we have greatly profited by its existence. From
time to time some assistance has to be given to them, but no Colony
has permanently been a charge upon the Empire. Every colony in the
Empire, in the long run, has been a profitable undertaking for the
Empire. . . .

. . . in spite of the difficulties in which these Colonies find themselves,
the West Indies at the present time take of British manufactures—not
foreign manufactures which come through Great Britain, but manufactures which have their origin in the United Kingdom—something
like three million pounds sterling per annum. . . .

Hansard 4s., 1898, 63, 875-78

(c) *House of Commons Speech, 2 August 1899*

Mr. J. Chamberlain: . . . we have already gone too far in that direction
:xtension of constitutional rights to the West Indies). As is shown by

the very small number of persons who take part in the elections, it is evident that the people who constitute the electorate do not care for the privilege, and the consequence is that these so-called liberal constitutions are really nothing more nor less than oligarchies. Under all these circumstances, I am convinced that a Crown Government which pays attention to such public opinion as exists in the colony is the best form of government possible.

Hansard 4s., 1899, 75, 1190

4 E. F. L. Wood[4] on his visit to the West Indies, 1922

Report

. . . neither in Jamaica nor elsewhere, is there any demand for responsible government in the strict sense of the word, nor within measurable distance of time could such a demand rightly be conceded. Though not the only ones, there are four principal considerations that are prohibitive. Notably in Trinidad, but to a considerable extent also in the other islands, the population is of various colour, religion and race. Great blocks of it are backward and politically undeveloped. For all this mosaic of humanity the Crown, through the Secretary of State, is in the position of responsible trustee: a responsibility of which it cannot morally divest itself until it is satisfied that it can delegate the charge to hands of not less certain impartiality or integrity than its own. Coloured and black well wishers of their own kind will tell you that that time is not yet.

Secondly, the absence of a class of leisured citizens who could take an active part in political life makes it necessary for the constitution to contain an element such as the official services supply, independent of local ties, and providing that detachment of outlook necessary for the effective conduct of the services controlled by Government. The comparative smallness and isolation of many of the islands make it questionable whether the experiment of responsible government would be practicable without a greater change in their economic position than their physical conditions seem to allow. Moreover, the conditions referred to involve the further risk, which is no small one, that the only effect of granting responsible government might be to entrench in power a financial oligarchy, which would entirely dominate the

---

4 Parliamentary Under-Secretary of State for the Colonies.

Colony and use their position for the sole purpose of benefiting one class instead of the community as a whole.

Thirdly, the controlling influence of the Secretary of State is essential for securing some uniformity of administration among these adjacent Colonies, whose actions must directly act and react on one another. If the fulness of time should ever lead to West Indian federation or anything analogous, this argument will disappear; but hitherto, the attempts to encourage West Indian unity have been slow and halting.

A fourth factor which makes 'responsible government' out of the question at the present stage of political development is the small proportion of the electorate who in fact exercise the franchise. Even in Jamaica, where interest in politics is most widely diffused, and where the press is very efficiently conducted, the number of registered voters who actually go to the poll is comparatively small. The majority of the Jamaican electors are coloured or negro small peasant proprietors, for the bulk of whom politics do not yet appear to be a matter of much concern. This limitation is even more forcibly evidenced in islands where the diffusion and standard of education are less advanced. In Dominica, for instance, about 70 per cent. of the population are illiterate, and in Trinidad, where educational standards are probably higher than in any other West Indian Colony, the average attendance at school of children of school age is only 56 per cent.

Given then on the one hand that the control of the Secretary of State must continue in effective form, and on the other that the movements towards elective representation must be met, it would seem clear that this can best be done by following existing precedents and including in the legislatures a certain number of members chosen by direct election. Details of the franchise for voters, of qualifications for members, important as they are, are subordinate to the main principle, and, if you lay down the general governing considerations, may best be discussed locally by the Government in conjunction with responsible persons of differing opinions. Similarly, there must be variation in the number of seats rendered available for elective representation. . . .

. . . But enough has been said to make it clear that the establishment of West Indian political unity is likely to be a plant of slow and tender growth. If any advance in this direction is to be achieved, it can only be as the result of a deliberate demand of local opinion, springing from the realisation of the advantages of co-operation under modern world conditions. Such development is likely only to be prejudiced, if ground were ever given for the fear that it was being imposed upon reluctant communities from without.

Having regard, therefore, to our experience, and to the universal doubts engendered by the very name of federation, I am satisfied that, so long as public opinion stands where it does to-day, it is both inopportune and impracticable to attempt amalgamation of existing units of government into anything approaching a general federal system.

Cmd 1679

5   Dr Shiels on conditions in the West Indies

House of Commons Speech, 22 May 1931

Dr. Shiels.[5]

. . . the constitutional questions . . . [are] a subject which we have been considering. . . . It seems reasonable, on the face of it, that some form of federation, either whole or partial, would be a desirable thing, but there are difficulties. There is in each island a large amount of local patriotism, and there is a disinclination to be linked up with other communities. There is also a considerable distance between many of the islands and although on a map you might think that they were very suitable for a federal system, on going into it more closely one can see that geography is not always helpful. It does appear, however, as if some form of group federation might be possible, where groups of islands might have more economical and efficient administration. That is one of the questions into which we are going at the present time. The Windward Islands . . . are one of the units which are being considered in connection with the question of the Federation of Trinidad and the Leeward and Windward Islands. We are trying to find out what the local opinion is on that subject, and to see if there is a *prima facie* case of getting some constitutional change of that kind. . . . I hope that we shall be able to arrive at a decision on the matter before too long.

. . . If there were time, I would have liked to tell the House how much has been done through the Colonial Development Fund, especially in the direction of carrying out some of the recommendations of the Olivier Report in connection with land settlement for smallholders— a line which seems to me one of the most hopeful in the West Indies. . . .

Hansard 5s., 252. 2483–5

[5] Under-Secretary of State for the Colonies.

VII

THE MEDITERRANEAN

The problems of a fortress area

Gibraltar and Malta were fortress colonies, and Cyprus an area of British administration since 1878. The Sultan of Turkey assigned Cyprus to be occupied and administered by Great Britain by a convention in that year which transferred full legislative power. The British Government was to pay the Porte 'whatever is the present excess of revenue over expenditure in the Island'. It formally annexed Cyprus on the outbreak of war with Turkey in 1914.

The Mediterranean was a combat area accustomed to strife, but after the opening of the Suez Canal in 1869, its use by merchant shipping lines increased. The constitution of Malta was liberal for a fortress colony, although 'Imperial interests' were closely safeguarded.

1 The British Government on the Constitution of Malta

(a) *House of Commons Statement, 28 July 1882*

Mr. E. Ashley:[1] . . . Efforts had been made for the improvement of the state of things in Malta both by the present and by the late Government; but the great difficulty that had to be contended with had lain in the constitution of the Legislative Council of Malta. . . . the franchise was too limited, and . . . the Members of the Council represented but a very small class of the population. All efforts at reform had been thwarted by the Council. The Colonial Office was so thoroughly convinced of that fact that they had determined that the Legislative Council should be placed upon a more liberal basis; and, accordingly, they had prepared a measure for that purpose; but they had thought it right that, before enlarging the franchise, they should submit to the Council the measure they proposed in order that the Council might express an opinion upon it. The difficulty in a proper constitution of the basis of the franchise was the education test difficulty. . . .

Hansard 3s., 1882, 273, 89–90

[1] Parliamentary Under-Secretary of State for the Colonies.

(b) *House of Commons Statement, 28 November 1882*

Mr. E. Ashley: . . . There has been every desire to regard the wishes of the Maltese people in respect of local affairs; and it is only in cases where it has been thought that Imperial interests were involved that the votes of the elected Members have been overruled by the official majority.

Hansard 3s., 1882, 275, 222

(c) *House of Lords Statement, 9 March 1883*

Earl of Derby:[2] . . . With regard to the Legislative Council, two matters were made the subject of complaint. One was that the elected Members were chosen on too narrow a basis; and the other that, from the composition of the Council, the elected Members were always outvoted by the official Members. With regard to the first of these complaints, he had dealt with it already. The number of electors was now, he believed, a little over 2,000; but by an arrangement already made, the Letters Patent having been granted, the suffrage would be extended to about a £6 rating. The effect of that would be to substitute some 6,000 electors for the 2,000 and odd who now held the franchise. That would not be considered a very revolutionary change, the total number of the inhabitants being upwards of 150,000. At the same time, it multiplied the present electoral body nearly three-fold, and was a substantial concession. With regard to the other and probably more important question, that of the powers which the Legislative Council exercised, he had thought it desirable to deal with that also. Undoubtedly, it was a fair ground of complaint if the elected Members of the Council were, on purely local matters, liable to be outnumbered and outvoted by an official body which gave its vote as one man. He had endeavoured to deal with that grievance by limiting the number of officials who should attend the meetings of the Council to a number equal to that of the non-official or elected Members, so that the two parties would exactly balance each other. He did not propose that the Governor should, as a general rule, vote at all; it was only in case of an exact balance of votes that he would give a casting vote. The Governor was directed that if the question was one, in his judgment, involving only local interests, and in which no Imperial interests were concerned, he was to accept the decision of the elected Members. If, on the other hand, Imperial matters were concerned, then the Governor might either suspend his decision, or, if he thought fit, he might outvote by his casting vote the elected Members. But, in case of his so doing, he

[2] Secretary of State for the Colonies.

was immediately to report the fact to the Secretary of State. The consequence would be that his powers would not be exercised except under the immediate supervision and control of the Colonial Office. He did not know whether that concession would satisfy all who had complained; possibly not; but it was a very large concession to their reasonable wants, and it would exhibit evidence of a desire to make local self-government in matters not affecting Imperial interests a reality and not a mere show. Another proposal was that, instead of all the electors voting in one constituency, the Island should be divided into electoral districts, seven or eight in number. That proposition had been inquired into. It was one which he saw no reason for opposing. It was a point on which local opinion and local feelings should be consulted, and he proposed to leave it to the Legislative Council to deal with as they might think fit. . . .

Hansard 3s., 1883, 276, 1887–8

(d) *House of Commons Statement, 14 March 1884*
Sir George Campbell asked the Under-Secretary of State for the Colonies. Whether anything has been done to relieve the poorer classes in Malta of the unequal taxes on food, as recommended by Her Majesty's Commissioner, Mr. Rowsell, some years ago?

Mr. Evelyn Ashley: Proposals for the diminution of the wheat tax have been brought before the Colonial Legislature; but they have been invariably opposed by the elected Members. In view of the declarations made by successive Secretaries of State, that the official majority shall not be used to override the elected Members in matters purely financial, and of mere local concern, Her Majesty's Government do not think it right to carry these proposals by that majority. The matter must now rest with the people of Malta themselves.

14 March 1884   Hansard 3s., 1884, 285, 1540–41

2   Churchill on the condition of Cyprus

Cabinet memorandum, 19 October 1907
. . . Although the most grinding economies were enforced, although all public works were neglected and the whole administration cut down to starvation point, we never succeeded, any more than the Sultan, in squeezing out of them the whole tribute of 92,800*l.*; and, in consequence of this, we proceeded to treat Cyprus as if she were a non-self-supporting Protectorate. She passed under the most rigid Treasury

control. The fruit of all economies, however self-denying, every surplus, however pitifully small, was seized at the end of each financial year; the difference between the amount collected and the cost of the administration and the whole tribute together was then voted as a grant-in-aid, and the accounts were presented to Parliament in a form which would lead any person to suppose that we were actually keeping Cyprus going out of British money. This iniquitous and immoral arrangement lasted for twenty-seven years, during which time we succeeded in extracting from this wretched island about 60,000l., a-year on the average, or about 1,600,000l. altogether.

At the beginning of 1906 the Colonial Office drew the attention of the Chancellor of the Exchequer to the lamentable condition of the island, to its slow progress under British rule, to the intolerable financial trammels in which it was held, and to the vicious system by which every local surplus or local economy only went to reduce the total of the grant-in-aid. The Chancellor then consented—and it was a liberal concession—to give what the Treasury call 'a fixed grant-in-aid of 50,000l. a-year', so that all economies or surpluses secured on that basis should enure to the profit of the island. In other words, we promised Cyprus that we would not make her contribute towards the payment of purely British debts more than 42,800l. in any one year. And this is the arrangement now in force, though be it not forgotten, lest generosity should go too far, it is an arrangement limited in its duration to three years.

. . . we have no right whatever, except by *force majeure*, to take a penny of the Cyprus tribute to relieve us from our own just obligations, however unfortunately contracted. There is scarcely any spectacle more detestable than the oppression of a small community by a great Power for the purpose of pecuniary profit; and that is, in fact, the spectacle which our financial treatment of Cyprus at this moment indisputably presents. It is in my opinion quite unworthy of Great Britain, and altogether out of accordance with the whole principles of our colonial policy in every part of the world, to exact tribute by force from any of the possessions or territories administered under the Crown. Let the figures be juggled by any sophistry or artifice within the wit of man, these two-root facts remain—that Cyprus pays 42,800l. a-year, and that Great Britain receives 42,800l. a-year for her own benefit, namely, to pay a portion of her own debts. And that, I say, constitutes a blemish upon Imperial policy of a peculiarly discreditable kind.

How different is the fate of Cyprus from that of any other island or Protectorate administered under the Colonial Office! To many of them we give large grants-in-aid—to Somaliland 76,000*l.* a-year—all dead loss to us, all clear gain to them. We are usually delighted to find them self-supporting. From none do we exact any payment, unless it be some contribution to the expense of the local garrison, by which they are defended, and by which they largely profit. But Cyprus, which came to us ruined and prostrate from centuries of horrible ill-usage: Cyprus which not only has never received a penny from us, but supports itself out of its own resources, and has contributed towards the payment of our debts a sum now amounting to 1,800,000*l.*, wrung out of her year by year at a cost of suffering and stagnation: Cyprus, because, forsooth, she cannot pay us more than 42,800*l.* a-year, is stigmatized as a pauper community living upon grants-in-aid.

. . . an island for which we are responsible, and which is administered as if it were a British Colony. . . . Every one knows that there is no present intention of altering the international status of Cyprus, and that we mean to go on occupying it indefinitely; and, in that case, surely it is time to drop the theory that we have only indirect responsibilities there, and that we have a right to do to Cypriotes things we would not dream of doing to our own fellow-subjects in any part of the British Empire. Let us recur to simple and sound foundations. Let us have only one measure for treating people subject to our rule, and that a measure of justice. Let us leave to the Island of Cyprus the whole of the revenues which are raised by the taxation of its people, to be expended on its own development, and to restore its once famous prosperity. Let us pay our own debts ourselves out of our own money. And let us choose next year, the thirtieth of our occupation, for that act of equity and reparation.

The present condition of the island is most unsatisfactory. I do not mean that it has not greatly progressed under our rule, still less that it is not incomparably better off than it would have been under Turkey; nor, indeed, that the Cypriotes themselves, Moslems and Christians alike, do not admit and recognise these facts. But an improvement upon Turkish standards is not a sufficient or suitable defence for British policy. The economic improvement and recovery of the island have been vastly extended. The annual drain, averaging between 20 and 30 per cent. of the total revenue, which has gone out of the island every year without any sort of return, has, when added to the necessarily costly character of high-class British administration, effectually prevented anything like a rapid recovery. . . .

It is well worth our while to make a success of Cyprus. Politically it is one of the countries where British methods are, so to speak, on trial before the tribunal of Europe. . . . from a purely material standpoint it is well worth our while to make a success of Cyprus, and easily within our power. I observe that we spend nearly 80,000*l.* a-year on the Somaliland Protectorate, which is almost totally unproductive; and even in other countries, now fed by grants-in-aid, there are highly speculative elements. But Cyprus is a certainty. We know that the island is already not only self-supporting, but able to contribute to our necessities a substantial sum . . . if the natural revenues of the island are allowed to be devoted to the necessary public works and scientific organization, this revival will assuredly take place with startling rapidity. Not only will Great Britain be vindicated by another good work of recuperation, but we shall find a more material reward in the preservation of a valuable area for British administrative capacity, and in the steady growth of trade connections. Whether the change which I propose would have the effect of dissipating the aspirations towards Greek national unity, which are beginning to cause so much disturbance, and will cause more, I cannot tell. . . .

In any case we should have done our duty, and have freed ourselves from a position which is morally, politically, and economically indefensible. . . .

W. S. C.[3]

19 October, 1907

Cab. 37/89/83

[3] W. S. Churchill, Parliamentary Under-Secretary of State for the Colonies.

E

VIII

BRITISH WEST AFRICA
Growth in African political experience

Growth in political experience of the African was the most significant development in British West Africa in these years. This occurred both through official channels, as with the introduction of elected Africans to the Nigerian Legislative Council in 1922, and through unofficial organisations such as the Aborigines Rights Protection Society or the National Congress of British West Africa. Experience in protest grew, especially through the channel of petition and the despatch of delegates to London.

Major political landmarks included the revocation of the Royal Niger Company charter, the annexation of Ashanti and the proclamation of a protectorate over the Northern Territories of the Gold Coast, and the amalgamation of northern and southern Nigeria.

1   The Berlin West Africa Conference

Despatch from Earl Granville[1] to Sir E. Malet[2]
(No. 59 Africa.)   *Foreign Office*
Sir,   *7 November 1884*
   I have to invite your Excellency's attention to the following observations which will serve generally for your guidance in the approaching Conference on West African questions.

   As regards the broad principles for the consideration of which the Conference is summoned, your attitude is clearly defined. Objects so completely in accordance with the consistent policy of this country as the freedom of commerce in the basin of the Congo, and of the navigation of the African rivers, should be warmly supported by you as Her Majesty's Representative. I have, however, to direct your attention to the consideration that commercial interests should not, in the opinion of Her Majesty's Government, be looked upon as exclusively the subject of deliberation; while the opening of the Congo markets is

---

[1] Secretary of State for Foreign Affairs.   [2] British Ambassador at Berlin.

to be desired the welfare of the natives should not be neglected; to them it would be no benefit, but the reverse, if freedom of commerce, unchecked by reasonable control, should degenerate into licence. Her Majesty's Government trust that this will be borne in mind, and that such precautions will be adopted for the regulation of legitimate commerce as may tend to insure, as far as possible, that its introduction will confer the advantages of civilization on the natives, and extinguish such evils as the internal Slave Trade, by which their progress is at present retarded. . . .

The position of the Niger is altogether different; on that river the establishment of a Commission is believed to be impracticable. The river itself, in a great part of its course, is very imperfectly explored, but it is known that it is divided geographically into three sections, the upper of which has no means of communication with the lower; the latter, when it approaches the sea, is split into a network of creeks little known and in many instances unsurveyed; the trade of the interior passes through the medium of coast tribes who act as middle-men and who, being keenly alive to their interests, are difficult to manage and control; the commerce owes its development almost exclusively to British enterprise: the trade is altogether in British hands; and the most important tribes, who have for years been accustomed to look on the agents of this country as their protectors and counsellors, have now, in consequence of their urgent and repeated appeals, been placed formally under the protectorate of Great Britain. On this river, therefore, a difference of application of the principles of the Congress of Vienna is imperative; the coast-line and lower course of the river are sufficiently under British control for Her Majesty's Government to be able to regulate the navigation, while binding themselves to the principle of free navigation by becoming parties to an International Declaration analogous to that contained in Article XV of the Treaty of Paris. . . .

F.O. 84/1814, p. 232

2 The Royal Niger Company

A former British army officer, Goldie, persuaded the main British companies trading on the lower Niger to merge in 1879 into the United African Company, known after 1882 as the National African Company. The activity of other European traders aroused fears lest they hamper the northward extension of British trade. In 1885 a Company agent secured from the Sultans of Sokoto and Gando treaties binding their people to trade only with the Company.

Since 1881 Goldie had pressed the British Government for a charter so that the Company might act as the Government's agent in keeping law and order in areas where it had treaties with local rulers. The Crown granted the charter in 1886, and the Company changed its name to the Royal Niger Company.

In 1899 the British Government decided that the Royal Niger Company should no longer be its agent in extending British influence in northern Nigeria. It revoked the charter, paid compensation and took over the Company's administrative and military assets in 1900.

Memorandum by the Chancellor of the Exchequer on the Royal Niger Company

Some months ago it was publicly intimated that Her Majesty's Government intended to make some change in the position of the Royal Niger Company. Ever since that intimation, Sir G. T. Goldie, on behalf of the Company, has been continually pressing on the Foreign Office, the Colonial Office, and latterly the Treasury, his views as to the nature of that change, and the position and claims of the Company. In these communications Sir G. T. Goldie has always assumed that there is no reason for any change in the position of the Company. He has claimed that those who founded and have managed it have allowed themselves to be actuated by patriotic motives to an extent detrimental to the commercial advantage of the shareholders; that there is no ground for the charge of 'monopoly' which has been brought against the Company by other British traders, and by foreigners; and he has stated that it has never sought to be bought out nor to have its Charter revoked. The position assumed is something more than that of an 'injured innocent', credit is claimed for operations which have potentially secured a large tract of Africa to British enterprise; and although the Company have neither defended their frontier against France, nor warned us that it was undefended, it is actually contended that the mere grant of the Charter binds us to go to war with France in defence of what the Company claim to be their rights, while they are to be at liberty to refuse to comply with our proposal that they should assert their rights by the occupation of certain important points in the territory in question.

. . . I cannot accept [this] view . . . as representing the actual facts. The Company's Charter expressly forbids a monopoly of the navigation and trade on the Niger. But they appear to me to have devoted their main efforts to securing a virtual monopoly of the river through their administrative system; and the loose wording of their Charter has enabled them to do this while keeping within its letter, though contravening its spirit. Sir G. T. Goldie contends that the only objectors to the proceedings of the Company in this respect are a few Liverpool traders, mainly interested in the sale of liquor. But it must be remembered that the Company has bought off objectors by absorbing other traders on the Niger, including some French and Germans; and it is obvious that this policy cannot be indefinitely continued. Their exaction from all persons, except their own members, of a 'trading licence' of 50l.; their prohibition against vessels touching, even for fuel, at any but forty specified points within a river length of 800 miles; their acquisition of the sole right to a strip of land along the river banks through the whole of its navigable course, giving them the power to compel outsiders to pay such a price as they may choose to fix for the establishment of trading stations, may have been necessary to the establishment and maintenance of the revenue from inland customs on which they depend, but are stated by Sir J. Kirk to be practically prohibitory of native trade on the Niger; and are not in accordance with the policy of freedom of commerce to which we are pledged by the Act of Berlin. The serious troubles with the Brassmen, and other matters, have shown how injurious this kind of action has been to their Colonial neighbours, and the present position of the Company could not be maintained in view of the proposals for freer navigation of the Niger which have been assented to by Her Majesty's Government in connection with the French negotiations, and which seem to me to be dictated rather by our general policy with respect to the navigation of such rivers as the Niger, than to be special concessions to France. I think, therefore, that having regard to the action of the Company on the Niger, it would have no equitable claim to any compensation for such an alteration in its Charter as would enable the policy of Her Majesty's Government with regard to the navigation of the Niger to be carried into effect, even though such an alteration might greatly affect the source from which much of the Company's revenue is now derived. If any such claim could be urged by the Company, it could only be on the ground that their Charter had been so carelessly drafted by the Foreign Secretary (Lord Salisbury) and Law Officers of the day, as to give them, unintentionally, a monopoly for the loss of which they ought to be compensated, an admission which I should be sorry to make to the House of Commons.

This, however, would not be an adequate solution of the matter. It appears to be agreed that it is essential in the interests of our Colonies that a common Tariff and a common Arms Law should be established throughout our whole maritime zone, and that all inland Customs frontiers should be abolished, while our relations with the French require that all administrative power in these regions should be exercised by the Crown. This amounts to the revocation of the Company's Charter. My own opinion has always been that before revoking the Charter we should settle with France, because until that is done we cannot tell what may be fairly due to the Company by way of compensation. It would, undoubtedly, be entitled to compensation for any rights to which, in our judgment, it is justly entitled and can legitimately exercise, but which, to suit our own convenience, or in return for other advantages, we might give up to France. But how can we ask Parliament to compensate it for the loss of an indefensible monopoly on the Niger, or to pay it for Treaty rights, many of which are, in the opinion of the Foreign Office, of very doubtful value, and some of which certainly could not be maintained? The Law Officers held that the Company has no general right to assign its Treaties, and that if it were dissolved, or reduced to the position of a mere trading Corporation, France might contend that its Treaties had lapsed; and they think it very undesirable that any change in the position of the Company, such as is suggested, should be made while the questions now pending with the French are unsettled. On the other hand, the Colonial Office press for military action in and near the Company's territories, and the Company, which could very largely reduce the cost of such action by aiding it, refuses to do so while its future is uncertain. I understood the Cabinet to agree that, on this ground, some definite proposal for purchase of its rights should now be made to the Company. For the reasons above stated, I thought it impossible to base such a proposal on any calculation of the value of the Company's rights, and I adopted, as the only practicable basis, the market price of the Company's shares at the date (5th October, 1897) at which the suggestion as to purchase was first put forward, plus an allowance for compulsory purchase. . . .

In estimating the proper addition for compulsory purchase, I have weighed the Company's services and its success in establishing relations with territories to the north-east of the Niger, especially the Empire of Sokoto, which undoubtedly may, in the future, be of great value to British trade, against the injury done to our negotiations with France by the Company's inaction with regard to Borgu, Gurma, and the districts to the north of these places, and the very precarious nature (to say the least) of the Company's revenue from customs duties on the Niger. The familiar addition of 10 per cent. seemed in all the circumstances a liberal allowance, and I, therefore, authorized Mr. Chamberlain to inform Sir G. Goldie that in return for the revocation of the Charter and the transfer of all the Company's property and rights to Her Majesty's Government, I was prepared to recommend Parliament to assume the Company's debt of 250,000*l*., and to pay it a further sum of 660,000*l*.—this latter sum to be subject to reduction by the valuation of any plant, buildings, or land, that it might be agreed that the Company should retain for trading purposes. . . .

M. E. H. B.[3]

February 21, 1898

Cab. 37/46/21

3   Lugard's preparations for an expedition against the Emir of Kano

Colonial Office memorandum for the Cabinet, 28 December 1902

In 1897 the French advanced north-east from Dahomey and down the Niger to Bussa. The British Government decided to aid the Company in facing the French Government troops, and agreed to provide money and officers for a West African Frontier Force. They entrusted the command to Lugard. In 1898 the British and French Governments agreed the western and northern boundaries of Nigeria.

The British Government, which was already paying for the defence of northern Nigeria, took over the administrative and military assets of the Company in 1900. It appointed Lugard to introduce British administration into the Protectorate of Northern Nigeria.

Sir Frederick Lugard has telegraphed to the Secretary of State for the Colonies to the effect that he has found it necessary to prepare an expedition against the Emir of Kano, which will start in the first days of January.

The force which he proposes to employ consists of 1,000 native troops, with 50 Europeans; they will have with them seven Maxim guns and five 75 mm. guns.

In reserve, Sir Frederick will have 680 native troops in three places; these will be armed with six Maxims, five 7-pr. R.M.L. guns, and one 75 mm. gun.

The force likely to oppose him is estimated at 4,000 horsemen and a large number of rabble.

The Emir is unpopular, and Sir Frederick does not anticipate that the majority of those in the field will fight. The Haussa population and the traders are on our side.

It has been determined to send a Commission to delimit the boundary between our territory and that of the French. This Commission

[3] The Chancellor of the Exchequer, Sir M. Hicks-Beach.

must be secured from attack, and communication must be maintained with it, in order to furnish it with supplies. Sir F. Lugard is of opinion that this can only be accomplished by the occupation of Kano.

The nearest British post to Kano is Zaria. On the 28th October last a force started from Kano to attack Zaria, but turned back on receiving the news of the death of the neighbouring Sultan of Sokoto.

The Emir of Kano has sent threatening messages to Captain Abadie, the Resident at Zaria, and has put a price upon his head; he is sheltering the murderer of Captain Moloney and his accomplices.

Sir F. Lugard has repeatedly testified to the fine qualities of the Fulah Sultans, or Emirs, in Northern Nigeria, and wherever a Fulah ruler has been deposed, another Fulah has been placed in his stead.

The Fulahs, however, are a conquering race. While the Haussas are traders, the Fulahs are horsemen and slave raiders.

Wherever we have deposed Fulah rulers, our advent has been received with rejoicing by the Haussas, as for example at Kontagora.

Bida is now perfectly quiet, as is Yola. Bautchi received our Resident without a shot being fired, and the Emir of Zaria has been friendly ever since we assisted him against the raids of the deposed Emir of Kontagora.

The Niger Company agreed to pay a subsidy to the Sultan of Sokoto, but, owing to the hostile attitude of this potentate, who refused to recognise the transfer to Great Britain, the Government has never paid the tribute; all these places, and others, where we are peacefully established, in former times paid a heavy tribute in slaves to the Sultan of Sokoto, as part of his empire, the tribute of Yola alone amounting to 10,000 per annum, and the Sultan has found this tribute cease from one Emir after another as our rule extended, which would sufficiently account for his hostility.

This expedition will not be carried out against the Haussa trading population, who are friendly to the Protectorate, but against their Fulani masters; it is therefore anticipated that Kano will settle down as quietly as has Bida, for the trade of the place will be encouraged.

The occupation of Kano was no part of the original plan for the protection of the Boundary Commissioners, but has been forced on us by the attitude of the Emir, which makes it unsafe to commence the delimitation under the conditions at present existing.

It is believed that the force which Sir F. Lugard proposes to employ is ample for the purpose, but I have given instructions to hold a reserve of 300 men each at Lagos, the Gold Coast, and Southern Nigeria.

As Sir Frederick Lugard believes the expedition to be absolutely necessary in the interests of humanity and self-preservation, and that to postpone it will inevitably be to invite attack under more dangerous conditions, while hesitation would endanger the allegiance of other States, who are fully aware of the attitude of the Emirs of Kano and Sokoto, I am not prepared to advise interference with the proposals of the High Commissioner or to forbid him to undertake the expedition. . . .

(FOR THE SECRETARY OF STATE.)
ONSLOW[4]

December 28, 1902

Cab. 37/64/3

4 Lugard Report

Report by Sir F. D. Lugard[5] on the amalgamation of Northern and Southern Nigeria, and administration, 1912–1919

8. *Nature of the Task.*—It was clear that so large a country as Nigeria, with an area of 332,400 square miles—of which the North and South were connected only by a single railway and the uncertain waterway of the Niger, while no lateral means of communication existed at all— must be divided into two or more dependent Administrations under the control of a Central Government. The first problem therefore which presented itself was the number of such Lieutenant-Governors, their powers, and relations to the various departments, together with the subordinate Administrative units throughout the country, and the control of such departments as the Railway and the Military Forces, which were common to the whole of Nigeria. The functions, and future constitutions, of the Executive and Legislative Councils, the unification of the Laws and the Regulations based upon them, and of the Executive 'General Orders' and other instructions, the Judicial system, the methods of Taxation direct and indirect, and the disposal of the Revenue so as to benefit the country as a whole, without creating jealousy and friction, the assimilation of the policy of Native Adminis- tration—these, with many minor problems, had to be solved by any scheme of amalgamation which should have any prospect of perman- ency. In every one of these matters the systems of the two Governments differed essentially. . . . The alarm and suspicion caused among the native population of the South by the appointment in England of a

---

[4] Parliamentary Under-Secretary of State, Colonial Office.
[5] Governor-General of Nigeria.

Committee to enquire into the question of land tenure added to the difficulty of the task. . . . The North—a younger Government—was capable of improvement in its departmental organisation, and backward both in the development of its material resources and of the facilities (such as roads) required for the purpose. The South required a better organisation of its Native Administration and of its judicial system. . . .

On January 1st, 1914, the former Governments of Southern and Northern Nigeria were formally amalgamated with some fitting ceremonial. After the oaths of office had been taken at each capital—Lagos and Zungeru—by the Governor-General, the Lieutenant-Governors, and the Chief Justice, etc., a Durbar was held on the great plain at Kano, which was attended by all the chief Moslem rulers from Sokoto to Chad, who met for the first time in common friendship to swear allegiance to His Majesty, and by representatives of the principal Pagan tribes. Though the retinue of the chiefs was necessarily limited by considerations of food supply, etc., it was estimated that not fewer than 30,000 horsemen took part in the picturesque display. Each in turn marched past and then gave the Salute of the Desert, charging at full gallop with brandished weapons. Nor was the gathering a mere ceremonial. Hereditary rivals met as friends. The Shehu of Bornu was the honoured guest of his quondam enemy, the Fulani Emir of Kano, and no friction or dispute for precedence among their somewhat turbulent following disturbed the harmony of this remarkable gathering, which undoubtedly had a very beneficial effect. . . .

. . . The whole of Nigeria—the size of which approximates to one-third that of British India, with a population of 16 or 17 millions, the largest of the Crown Colonies and Protectorates of the Empire—was placed under the control of a Governor-General, but it was intimated that the title was personal to myself. . . .

9 April, 1919   Cmd 468

5   The Gold Coast Native Affairs Department

Gold Coast Government report, 1920

One of the most striking events of the year was the formation by certain educated Natives of the several West African Colonies of the body know [sic] as the National Congress of British West Africa which sent a deputation to England to represent their political aspirations. Considerable opposition to their action arose among some of the inland Chiefs and people whom the Congress professed to represent. The year ended before they had returned to West Africa to give an account of their mission.

C.O. 98/34

6 Petition of the National Congress of British West Africa

1. That your Petitioners are the accredited representatives of the National Congress of British West Africa, which was brought into being after the first Conference of Africans of British West Africa . . .

2. . . . the policy of the Congress is 'to preserve strictly and inviolate the connection of the British West African Dependencies with the British Empire and to maintain unreservedly all and every right of free citizenship of the Empire and the fundamental principle that taxation goes with effective representation.'

7. That your Petitioners desire to bring to the notice of Your Majesty that the administrations of the several British West African Dependencies are composed of Executive and Legislative Councils. The Members of the Executive Councils are all Government officials who also together with Members nominated by the Governors compose the Legislative Councils. As such the nominated Members do not really represent the people, and they are not directly in touch with them.

11. . . . the National Congress of British West Africa represents substantially the intelligentsia and the advanced thought of British West Africa, . . . it also represents the bulk of the inhabitants of the various indigenous communities . . .

12. . . . the principle of electing representatives to local councils and bodies is inherent in all the systems of British West Africa which are essentially Democratic in nature. . . .

13. That, further, according to the African system no Headman, Chief, or Paramount Ruler has an inherent right to exercise Jurisdiction unless he is duly elected by the people to represent them, and that the appointment to political offices also entirely depends upon the election and the will of the people.

14. That such being the British West African System of representation, the arrangement by which the Governor of a Crown Colony nominates whom he thinks proper to represent the people cannot but

strike them as a great anomaly and does constitute a grievance and a disability which they now respectfully pray may be remedied.

15. That it is consequently desired that the people may be given the opportunity of electing one-half of the Members of the Legislative Council, the other half being nominated by the Crown besides the power of electing six other financial representatives to a House of Assembly, who, together with the Members of the Legislative Council, shall have the power of imposing taxes and of discussing freely and without reserve the items on the annual estimates of revenue and expenditure prepared by the Governors in the Executive Council and approving of them, and that the advantage of the reform herein advocated be extended to both the European and African Members of the various British West African communities.

16. That there is present in indigenous institutions a method of electing representatives. But it is submitted that where such indigenous institutions do not provide a ready means of ascertaining the will of the people, other qualifying methods for voting, such as property or an educational standard, may be resorted to. . . .

20. That Your Majesty's Petitioners would further draw attention to the urgent need there is for separating judicial functions from those of the Executive. . . .

24. . . . the time has come for the establishment of Municipal Corporations in all the principal towns of British West Africa with full power of local self-government, and that the people may have the power of electing four-fifths of the Members thereof and the remaining one-fifth nominated by the Government, such elected and nominated members having the power of electing the Mayor of the Corporation, who, however, must be an elected member.

25. That your Petitioners desire the establishment of a British West African University, and are prepared to promote the necessary funds for its establishment, supported by Government subsidies. . . .

27. That your Petitioners view with marked disfavour the scheme of the Empire Resources Development Committee. . . . In this connection, it is submitted that the principle of Trusteeship may easily be made to operate detrimentally to African proprietary rights, and that the people are well able to control their own lands and to watch and protect their proprietary interests. . . .

30. That your Petitioners desire to draw attention to the dangerous practice of trying without a jury persons charged with offences, particularly capital offences. . . .

32. That Your Majesty's Petitioners view with grave alarm the

right assumed by the European Powers of exchanging or partitioning African countries between them without regard to the wishes of the people, and beg leave respectfully to request that the partitioning of Togoland between the English and the French be reconsidered. . . .

Signed for and on behalf of the National Congress of British West Africa . . . by the Honourable T. Hutton-Mills, The Honourable Casely Hayford, Edward Francis Small, Henry Maurice Jones, Frederick W. Dove, Dr. H. C. Bankole-Bright, H. Van Hein and J. Egerton-Shyngle and by Amo du Tijani, Chief Oluwa. . . .

19th October, 1920   C.O. 98/33

7 Colonial Office reply to the petition

DOWNING STREET,
26TH JANUARY, 1921

Sir,

I am directed by Viscount Milner to acknowledge the receipt of your letter dated the 30th of October last in which was enclosed a petition signed by yourself and eight other persons on behalf of 'The National Congress of British West Africa.'

2. Lord Milner has laid the petition before the King and has received His Majesty's commands to reply to it.

3. His Lordship has received from the Governors of Nigeria and the Gold Coast information which shows that 'The National Congress of British West Africa' is in no way representative of the native communities on whose behalf it purports to speak, that its pretensions in this respect are expressly repudiated by the most authoritative exponents of native public opinion (including practically all the Chiefs in the Gold Coast), and that the scheme put forward by the Congress would in their opinion be inimical to the best interests of the community. Lord Milner has no reason to suppose that any different opinion is held in Sierra Leone or the Gambia.

4. The Secretary of State has, however, carefully considered the petition, and as a result His Lordship has advised the King that the time has not yet come for the introduction into any of the West African Colonies and Protectorates of the principles of election to the Legislative Councils and of unofficial majorities on those Councils. Nor does he consider that the legal changes suggested in the petition would

improve the administration of justice and be in the interest of the great bulk of the native populations. He has accordingly been unable to advise His Majesty to grant the prayers of the petitioners on these points.

5. Of the other matters referred to in the petition, some relate to all the British West African Colonies and Protectorates, some to only one or two, while their relative importance varies greatly. With regard to these matters, the Secretary of State will consult the Governors of the several Colonies concerned. . . .

I am, etc.,

H. J. READ.[6]

H. C. BANKOLE BRIGHT ESQ.

C.O. 98/33

8 The Gold Coast

Governor's Speech at the Legislative Council, 27 April 1921

My first reason is in connection with the duty of the Government to weigh the balance carefully between all sections of the community.

In this case we have two parties to deal with. On one side, a body of men, elected at a Conference of persons representing four British Colonies, and claiming to represent all the people in the Gold Coast. On the other side, we have an important paramount chief of this country, supported in the Chamber by another paramount chief and all the unofficial native members of the Legislative Council representing influential sections of the community, stating that this body of men does *not* represent the whole of the people of the Gold Coast. . . .

I have heard a good deal from the speakers about the general progress of the Conference which afterwards developed into the Congress. I would now like to draw the attention of Honourable Members to certain plain facts showing the extent to which the Government was aware of what was going on. I shall epitomise these plain facts under six events.

The first was the assembling of a Conference of natives of all British West Africa in Accra in the Spring of 1920. This Conference met to discuss points for the good of the various countries in West Africa. It was welcomed by this Government, as well as by the Governors of all the other colonies, and the latter, including myself, sent telegrams wishing the Conference well. . . . The Government welcomed this

[6] Assistant Under-Secretary of State, Colonial Office.

Conference because it is its declared policy to find out as far as possible what the people want. . . .

The second event was the arrival at Government headquarters of the Resolutions of the Conference with a request that we should send them up to the Secretary of State. We did so, and they were acknowledged.

I was interested to see amongst the more important of these Resolutions that there was scarcely one in which I had not, since my arrival in this country, invited the co-operation and confidence of the African Members of Council and other leading citizens of the Gold Coast.

The third event was the receipt of another set of Resolutions, this time from the Secretary of the London Committee. It was dated the 21st September 1920, and was our first intimation that the Secretary of State was to be memorialised. . . .

The fourth event was the receipt by this Government for the first time of information that the delegates in London were memorialising His Majesty the King. The letter was dated 30th October in London. It reached here towards the end of November . . . we were thus not informed until after the event had taken place.

The fifth event was the protest to which I have already alluded, made by two prominent paramount chiefs of this country in this chamber on the 30th December last. The protest was made by the Honourable Nana Ofori Atta . . . strongly supported by the late Honourable Nana Amonoo V, by the Honourable Dr. Quartey-Papafio and the Honourable E. J. P. Brown . . . although it may be said to have been unfortunate that there was no Honourable Member present, to represent the Congress or its opinion, that was not the fault of the Honourable Nana Ofori Atta, who wished to defer his speech, but it was at my express wish that he gave it.

The sixth event was a telegram sent by me to the Secretary of State for the Colonies. . . .

. . . Here we have a body of men proceeding to Europe claiming that they represented all the people or practically all the people of this country. On the other hand we have two of the important paramount chiefs protesting that they did not represent them. They were supported by two other Honourable unofficial native members. . . .

C.O. 98/35

SOUTHERN AFRICA
Sovereignty and paramountcy

The years from 1880 to 1932 in southern Africa saw decisions on sovereignty, suzerainty, bestowal of allegiance, acceptance of superior might and character of administration. There were transfers of effective government. Extensive political change was accompanied by change in the economic sphere, in composition of population and nature of communications. The Anglo-Boer war of 1899–1902 was followed in 1910 by a major political merger—the Union of South Africa. Once this Union was formed, Europeans strove to assert or maintain political predominance over non-Europeans, giving stronger legislative form to this policy as modernisation of South Africa advanced, and movement of population became both more necessary in response to industrial needs, and easier.

North of the territories which had become the Union, the British Government had assumed sovereignty but evaded the burden of administration by the device of a chartered company. The years saw this company wield control over extensive regions, only to yield up administrative authority after the first world war.

The High Commission Territories: the colony of Basutoland and the protectorates of Bechuanaland and Swaziland

The British Government annexed Basutoland in 1868 after the paramount chief Moshesh had repeatedly asked for protection. In 1871 it was incorporated in Cape Colony, but in 1883 the British Government resumed administration as a result of agitation on behalf of the Basutos and to protect African land rights. The Secretary of State Lord Derby told the Cape Government that the British Government accepted 'no permanent responsibility for the affairs of this part of South Africa'. The High Commissioner for South Africa governed it under direct British rule.

The British Government declared the whole of Bechuanaland a protectorate in 1885. They then decided to establish the crown colony of British Bechuanaland south of the Molopo River, leaving the region between that river and the twenty-second parallel of south latitude a protectorate. It was the Cabinet who decided on the twenty-second parallel, and the Colonial Office thought they intended mainly to meet the fear of German annexation between the west coast and the Transvaal, and to secure the main trade route north from filibusters. An Order in Council in 1891 authorised the High Commissioner for South Africa to exercise jurisdiction in the protectorate. The crown colony of British Bechuanaland was incorporated in Cape Colony in 1895.

In Swaziland the granting of extensive concessions to Europeans made European control necessary in the 1880s. A joint administration set up by the British and Transvaal governments in 1890 proved unworkable, and in 1894 the Transvaal took over control. After the South African war of 1899–1902 Swaziland was placed under British administration, and in 1906 was brought under the direct control of the High Commissioner for South Africa.

1 Basutoland

Colonial Office memorandum, 18 November 1880

Basutoland is an inland territory stretching in a north-easterly direction from the old borders of the Cape Colony to the borders of Natal. . . .

The latest statistics give its inhabitants as:

Europeans	469
Natives	127,707

The natives are a mixed race of Basutos, Bushmen, Tambookies, Fingoes, and Zulus, the pure Basutos predominating.

. . . The Cape Act 12 of 1871 provided that Basutoland should, from a date to be proclaimed by the Governor, form part of the Colony of the Cape of Good Hope, but that it should not by virtue of such annexation become subject to the general law of the Colony.

The power of making laws, rules, and regulations for Basutoland was vested in the Governor for the time being, and it was declared that no Act of the Cape Parliament should be deemed to extend to Basutoland, unless extended thereto by express words in the Act itself, or some other Act, or by notice or proclamation of the Governor, containing express words for the purpose. Another provision of the Act empowered the Colonial Courts to take cognizance of matters declared by the Governor to be cognizable by them.

The existing code of law for Basutoland is contained in a proclamation of Sir Henry Barkly, issued under the powers conferred by the Act, and dated the 29th of March 1877. It contains simple provisions as to the magistrates, courts, crimes, punishments, civil disputes, marriage, land, hut tax, passes, pounds, posts, and other matters of chief local importance. In civil cases where all the parties are natives, native law is made the rule of justice, where it is otherwise the law of the Cape Colony is made the rule.

There is a Chief Magistrate in Basutoland, who is also the Governor's Agent, and six subordinate magistrates.

Some thousands of the people are Christians, and many others of them have, in deference to Missionary influence, adopted Christian customs to a certain extent.

Every year the magistrates and people meet in a sort of informal parliament, where politics are talked and grievances stated. The general tone at these meetings has been that of profound loyalty and gratitude to the English Government.

In the year following that in which Basutoland was annexed to the Cape, the Cape itself, at the instance of the Home Government, accepted the system of what is called responsible government. Since 1850 there had been a parliament, and the change effected in 1872 consisted in the substitution of the leaders of the parliamentary majority for permanent officials in the chief executive offices. In New Zealand, the concession of responsible government to the Colonists, was subjected at first to a reservation to the Governor, acting upon his personal responsibility, of a certain control over native policy.[1] Sir Henry Barkly, before proceeding to assume the government of the Cape in 1870, asked the Secretary of State for the Colonies whether he was, in the event of responsible government being carried, and of Basutoland being annexed to the Cape, to exercise any similar authority; and Lord Kimberley's reply was in the negative.

. . . Basutoland was annexed to the Cape, and, responsible government being adopted in that Colony, the Basutos ceased to 'depend from the High Commissioner', and became subject to the political control of the representatives of the majority in the Cape Parliament. For six years this made little difference. Sir Henry Barkly exercised a strong but unobtrusive influence in native affairs, and the general policy of his ministers was in no way at variance with his own. . . .

Signed,
E.F. (EDWARD FAIRFIELD)[2]

18 November 1880

Cab. 37/4/73

---

[1] The arrangement was afterwards abandoned as unworkable.
[2] First class clerk in the Colonial Office.

2 Facts relating to the Swazi Crisis

Colonial Office memorandum, 19 May 1894

What may be called the permanent rights and obligations of Her Majesty's Government and of the Government of the South African Republic in regard to Swaziland are contained in Sections 12 and 2 of 'The Convention of London, 1884', by which (1) both Powers recognize the independence of the Swazis, (2) the South African Republic undertakes to conclude no Treaty with native tribes east or west of the Republic—a definition including Swaziland—without the approval of Her Majesty's Government, and (3) Her Majesty's Government takes power to appoint, if necessary, Commissioners in the native territories on the east and west of the Republic 'to maintain order and prevent encroachments'. . . . between 1884 and 1890 the Swazis were more or less left to themselves, until the growing confusion in the country led the two Governments to conclude the Swaziland Convention of 1890, which, while reaffirming the independence of the Swazis, provided for the establishment of a Government Committee, 'with the consent of the Swazis', to rule over the whites. This Committee consisted of a triumvirate, being composed of a nominee of each Government, together with Mr. Theophilus Shepstone, C.M.G., who had for some time been acting as 'Adviser' of the Swazi nation. The natives were nominally left to govern themselves. . . .

The Convention of 1890, which was only concluded for three years certain, was duly denounced by the South African Republic about a year ago. . . . in the meantime, Her Majesty's Government, in view of the hopes held out by the late Government to the South African Republic when negotiating the Convention of 1890, had consented to conclude what is now known as the Convention of 1893 [by which] the South African Republic was permitted, subject to certain safeguards affecting the rights of the Swazis and of British subjects, to obtain by negotiation from the Swazis an 'Organic Proclamation' or other Instrument (to be approved by Her Majesty's Government), conferring on the Republic powers of jurisdiction, protection, and administration.

The term 'Organic Proclamation' . . . means a public legislative declaration by the Swazi Sovereign in Council, conferring what may be called constitutional or administrative rights on some persons or corporation . . . it is owing to the determined refusal of the Swazis to sign the new Organic Proclamation, framed by the South African Republic, and approved by Her Majesty's Government, for giving effect to the Convention of 1893, that the present crisis has arisen. Such opposition was not in the least anticipated by President Krüger, and not seriously apprehended on our side. . . .

C. O., 19 May, 1894
Cab. 37/36/16

3   The Swazi Crisis

Colonial Office memorandum, 18 May 1894

Serious difficulties have arisen in Swaziland in regard to the bringing into operation of the Convention entered into last year between us and the South African Republic . . . It is a condition of that Convention that the Organic Proclamation . . . should be freely agreed to by the Swazi Queen-Regent and Council; but great opposition has sprung up in Swaziland to any administration of the country by the Boers, and there appears at present very little chance of any Organic Proclamation founded upon the Convention of 1893 being accepted by the native authorities. It is difficult to say how far this opposition is genuine. The Swazis . . . do not, or will not, understand to what an extent their rights of administration have been given away by the concessions of the late King. I have no doubt that certain English concessionaires, in the hope of being bought out by the South African Republic, are exciting the natives to resist the entrance of the Boers, and I have a strong suspicion that the Boers themselves are not really anxious that the Organic Proclamation should be accepted, thinking that, if troubles arise in consequence of its refusal, they will get possession of Swaziland without any of the restrictions for the protection of the natives which the Convention of 1893 imposes. But it cannot be denied, I think, that there is a great dislike of Boer rule among the Swazis, and that they would much prefer to be annexed by us. They have during the recent negotiations frequently offered their country to the Queen, and they seem incapable of understanding the reason, viz., our Treaty obligations to the South African Republic, which prevents their offer from being accepted. For the moment, therefore, there is a deadlock. The present form of administration, established by the Convention of 1890, terminates with that Convention on the 30th June next; the new system embodied in the Convention of 1893 cannot come into operation till the Organic Proclamation has been accepted by the Swazi Queen-Regent and Council, and their acceptance is withheld. . . .

. . . It must also be remembered that a feeling exists in this country against what is called 'handing over the Swazis to the Boers' not only amongst philanthropists, but among Chambers of Commerce and bodies of that kind. I do not attach much importance to their opinions upon such a subject as this, knowing how they are manufactured; but in the case of a Swazi war, they would count against us.

. . . I hope that the Cabinet will be willing to consider the matter at its next meeting, as the earliest possible decision as to the policy to be adopted is most desirable.

(Signed)   RIPON.[3]

May 18, 1894

Cab. 37/36/15

4   Swaziland

Memorandum by the Imperial Secretary to the High Commissioner for South Africa, 1 February 1895

. . . That Organic Proclamation, owing mainly to the intrigues of agitators, has not been and will not be signed, and it has thus been found impossible to realise the hopes then formed of Swazi consent.

Her Majesty's Government had therefore to face the difficulty of yielding the condition of Swazi consent or of allowing the country to drift into anarchy.

. . . It was evident that, owing to the ignorance and blind obstinacy of the Swazi Queens, the Swazies would never consent to any practicable Treaty, and Her Majesty's Government have therefore adopted the only course available, namely, to recognise the title of the South African Republic to control Swazi affairs, but subject to their consenting to the best terms obtainable in a new Convention, which contemplates the continued refusal of the Swazi consent.

That Convention secures to the Swazies everything of value that they have not themselves already alienated. It protects British and native interests and secures the honest administration of justice. It also provides for the appointment of a British Consular officer.

. . . it only remains to consider the alternative courses.

A British Protectorate is legally impossible, politically undesirable, and geographically impracticable.

[3] Secretary of State for the Colonies.

It is legally impossible because it could not be legally established without the consent of the Government of the South African Republic.

It is politically undesirable because it would involve a perpetual charge on Imperial funds—all the sources of revenue having been alienated and the alienation confirmed by the Concession Court; moreover it would be a perpetual source of irritation, weakness, and anxiety, hampering our future policy in South Africa.

It is geographically impracticable because we have no practicable means of access to the country.

A continuance of the joint Government is in itself undesirable and also impossible. It is undesirable because a dual Government never works smoothly, and it is only by mutual trust and concession that it can be made to work at all. It is creditable to both the British and Transvaal representatives that the system has lasted so long, but it certainly could not last any longer, even if the Transvaal Government would agree to continue it, which it will not do, and an *Alsatia* is impossible—the fourth possible course.

There remains therefore the present Convention, and although there may be some who entertain feelings hostile to the Transvaal administration, nevertheless all must admit that it is infinitely preferable to the Swazi native system of wholesale killing off, of smelling out, and of eating up. Moreover it provides the greatest of all safeguards—an honest Court, the Supreme Court of the Transvaal, of which the reputation for an untarnished administration of justice is unquestionable.

Finally it may be said that the policy adopted has received the approval of practically the whole of the European public opinion of British South Africa.

GRAHAM BOWER[4]

1st February, 1895

Cab. 37/38/11

5 Proposed incorporation of Bechuanaland with the Cape Colony

Colonial Office memorandum, 20 June 1895

Both Houses of the Cape Parliament have passed Resolutions in favour of the transfer of the Crown Colony of Bechuanaland to the

---

[4] Imperial Secretary to High Commissioner for South Africa.

Cape Colony. The Resolutions were proposed by the Cape Government, and there was practical unanimity in their favour. It is therefore now necessary that we should consider what answer should be given to them. . . . It would, I suppose, be generally admitted that the ultimate destination of the Crown Colony of Bechuanaland is annexation to the Cape Colony. The only question is one of time and opportunity.

It seems to me that so far as the Colonial aspects of the matter are concerned, there are several strong arguments in favour of acceding to the wishes of the Cape Parliament.

In the first place we should by doing so relieve the Imperial Exchequer from an expenditure which, on sound principles, ought not to fall on it. We should secure for the Crown Colony a more efficient administration of justice than it now possesses or is likely to get at Imperial cost. And, lastly, I believe that we could at the present moment, in consequence of Mr. Rhodes's eagerness for the proposed annexation, obtain easily better terms for the natives from the Cape than we should be likely to get hereafter if this opportunity is lost. I should propose to stipulate with the Colony that the land rights of the natives should be respected, that their Reserves should be maintained, that the existing laws and regulations as to the liquor traffic should be retained, and that the Glen Grey Act should not be applied to Bechuanaland without the consent of the Secretary of State. I should also require the Colony to enter into satisfactory arrangements for the position and pension rights of the Officers now employed by the Imperial Government in the administration of the Crown Colony. I have every reason to believe that the Cape Government in their present temper would accept these terms.

But the question has, of course, to be looked at from another point of view. The transfer of the Crown Colony to the Cape may be objected to in Parliament by Sir Ellis Ashmead-Bartlett, Mr. Arnold Forster, and other Members of the Opposition of more importance, and some persons believe by Mr. Chamberlain as well. Mr. Buxton thinks that this opposition might be serious, and would certainly involve some consumption of time, and would therefore prefer to delay our decision. He is, of course, a better judge than I can be of what is likely to happen in the House of Commons, but I deprecate delay because I fear that if we do not make use of the present occasion the Cape Government are likely to get cold in the matter, and our chance of making really good terms both for the natives and for our officers will be seriously diminished. I should insist upon those terms; if we cannot get them, I should refuse to agree to the transfer—but if they are given, as I think that they would be, it would be a mistake to let slip the present opportunity of making a satisfactory and final settlement of this long-pending question.

R.[5]

20.6.95

Cab. 37/39/36

6 Zululand

GENERAL VIEW OF ZULU AFFAIRS, 1879–1885

The Settlement of 1879

From a period closely following the conclusion of the Zulu War in August 1879, the state of Zululand has given rise to anxiety both on the part of Her Majesty's Government and on that of the Natal Government. But the conditions of the problem have been continuously changing, and whilst some causes of anxiety have disappeared, others have arisen in their stead, and it therefore remains to discover and adopt a policy towards Zululand which may be consistent with justice towards the local interests concerned, as well as to those of an Imperial nature.

As the phases of the difficulty have changed so often and so materially, it will suffice to run over the earlier history of Zululand since the war, very rapidly.

The settlement of Zululand, effected by Lord Wolseley, under the authority of Lord Beaconsfield's Government, was one of those arrangements which would have worked well if everybody concerned had been anxious that it should work, and determined that he himself would behave properly; but this was not the case. Powerful combinations, inside and outside Zululand, arose which ignored the settlement, or worked for its overthrow. The thirteen chiefs amongst whom the country was divided, proved unable to maintain a stable peace: some of them were neither powerful nor popular, and it is only a powerful or popular chief who can command obedience among Zulus. The settlement itself made no provision for the vindication of authority in the contingencies which arose. The Government of Mr. Gladstone was unwilling to take the responsibility of departing from the scheme of Lord Beaconsfield's Government and interfering directly to preserve order—a policy recommended by Sir Evelyn Wood, then acting as Governor of Natal. . . .

[5] The Secretary of State for the Colonies, Lord Ripon.

. . . The Zulus knew they were giving away part of their country, and Mr. Grant told them as much, but whether he told them or knew himself what proportion of their country they were giving away is improbable. The Boers certainly at first, and probably to the last, represented the land cession as consisting of the old 'Disputed Territory' on the Utrecht border. . . . Nobody knows what is the size of Zululand, and therefore what is the proportion borne by this grant to the whole. . . . Even if the deed was interpreted to them, it is impossible to suppose that they had any idea of how much they were giving away, or that they were not leaving themselves (as Sir Henry Bulwer now surmises) enough to live on comfortably. By a telegram dated the 26th of December we learn that the Boers have now taken five-sixths of Zululand beyond the Reserve. . . .

Future Policy

. . . if it is thought necessary to interfere, the right to do so is unquestionable. It was a term in the conditions imposed on every one of the thirteen chiefs appointed after the Zulu war that he was not to 'sell, or in any way alienate or permit or countenance any sale or alienation of any part of the land in' his territory; and the same stipulation was agreed to by Cetywayo as one of the terms of his restoration (p. 114 of C—3466), as well as one providing that the succession to the Zulu throne after his death should be subject to the approval of the British Government. The British Government has neither assented nor objected to the succession of Dinuzulu; but even if his succession be acknowledged, it is obvious that his rights are subject to a treaty disability to alienate his land, which the British Government may or may not insist on, as it sees fit, against third parties having notice of the disability.

By a telegram of the 4th of January 1886, the New Republic has been warned that Her Majesty's Government cannot regard the survey of farms in Zululand or their occupation as conferring any valid title, or as in any way affecting existing rights of the Zulu tribes or Her Majesty the Queen, and that Her Majesty's Government cannot view with indifference any course of action tending to bring on disturbances near the Zulu Native Reserve. The correspondence on the subject has been published, with the sanction of the Secretary of State, in the Natal *Gazette*, and is therefore now widely known throughout South Africa.

With regard to the policy of Mr. Gladstone's Government towards Zululand, it may be observed that whilst its declarations against intervention were constant up to the time of the Boer intervention, and the adoption of a colonial policy by Germany, after the effects of those events had developed themselves, their views appeared to undergo a certain degree of modification, as may be inferred from the following answer of Mr. Gladstone's in the House, of the 14th of November, 1884; 'The attention of the Government is being directed to the condition of Zululand, with the view of considering the question whether these obligations of honour or policy are involved in an interference in its affairs. The moment they see that the time for such interference has arrived, they will deem it their duty to make it known to the House'....

C.O., January 1886   Cab. 37/17/18

7   The Constitution of Natal

(a) *Colonial Office memorandum, 8 May 1880*
Natal is a Colony possessing representative institutions without responsible government. The Imperial Government has the control of public officers, as in a Crown Colony; but laws are made by a Legislative Council consisting partly of elected and partly of official and nominated members, and the Crown has no more than a veto on legislation.

The charter of 1856, erecting Natal into a distinct and separate Colony, is the basis of the present constitution. Certain important modifications . . . have been introduced as occasion arose in respect of the composition of the Executive and Legislative Councils and the amount of the Reserved Civil List; but they have not been such as to transfer Natal from the class of Colonies intermediate between Crown Colonies and those possessing responsible government.

By the Charter of 1856 the administration of Natal was entrusted to a Governor or Lieutenant-governor assisted by an Executive Council, and a Legislative Council composed of four official members and 12 members elected by the counties and boroughs. The qualification of electors was declared to be the possession of any immoveable property of the value of 50*l.*, or the occupation of any such property of the yearly value of 10*l.* The reserved civil list was fixed at 8,750*l.*

From the first, therefore, the elected members of the Legislative Council have had it in their power to thwart the proposals of the Executive Government, while on the other hand they have not had sufficient power to make them feel adequate responsibility for the results of their action. The difficulty of working such a constitution would in any case be great. In Natal it is enhanced by the fact that the majority of the Legislative Council represents the white population alone, which . . . (amounted) in 1876 to 22,759 as against 316,711 natives and 17,047 coolies. The white population in fact, which alone is represented in the Council, has throughout been little more than $\frac{1}{15}$th of the whole population of the Colony . . . even in prosperous and quiet times the Government has too often had to yield to the irresponsible opposition of the elected members. . . .

The Legislative Council, in anticipation of the 23rd September, have passed an address to the Queen praying for Responsible Government. . . .

The objections to granting responsible Government are:

1. That a community of little more than 20,000 persons of European origin is necessarily unable to provide the materials for a system of Parliamentary Government, with a Legislature of two chambers, which would apparently derive its authority from an electorate of about 4,000 persons, of whom only 1,000 exercised the franchise on the last occasion.

2. That it would be neither justifiable nor safe to entrust to 22,300 European colonists the rights and interests of nearly 400,000 natives who have made little progress in civilisation and still live under native laws and tribal organisations, and of a coolie population nearly equal to that of European descent.

3. That it is a principle of Colonial policy that the right of self-government involves the duty of self-defence, which means not only the maintenance of internal order, but defence against aggression from bordering native tribes; but that it appears to have been very generally admitted in the Legislative Council, either directly or implicitly, that the Colony could do very little towards providing for this latter branch of its duty. . . .

R. L. A.[6]

May 8, 1880.   Cab. 37/2/22

(b) *Colonial Office memorandum, 23 October 1891*

The question for consideration is whether the Responsible Government Bill, which has been reserved, should be sanctioned or disallowed. No Imperial legislation is necessary to effect the change.

In 1882 Her Majesty's Government offered to grant Responsible Government to Natal, if the Colonists, after a General Election, decided in favour of it.

Her Majesty's present Government are not absolutely pledged to

[6] R. L. Antrobus, Clerk in the Colonial Office.

give Responsible Government to the Colony, but, as the correspondence shows, the people have been led to understand that if proper protection is secured to the Natives, we are in favour of granting it.

I believe the change is very desirable—

1st. Because the present form of Government (representative but not responsible) is objectionable, and has led, and will lead, to difficulties. It throws responsibility upon the Home Government by vesting in it the control of the Public Officers, while giving it no power of carrying its measures, or of obtaining supplies, so that its control is merely nominal; and experience has shown that it cannot be exercised without giving rise to a deadlock.

Sir C. Mitchell, who has served for many years in Natal as Colonial Secretary and is now Governor, states that in his opinion the Colony has entirely outgrown its present form of Government, and that Natal should adopt a system under which those possessing the power of control will be made responsible for its exercise.

This, it may be observed, was the principal reason for doing away with a similar Constitution in Western Australia, and granting Responsible Government; and the reason was approved unanimously by Parliament.

2nd. Because the grant of Responsible Government will place Natal in a better position in South Africa as regards the Cape Colony and the two Republics.

Sir C. Mitchell reports that he has no doubt that Natal has suffered, and is suffering, from want of political equality with those communities.

It may be added that, assuming federation in South Africa to be desirable, this change would distinctly tend to promote it.

The first question to be considered is whether the change is desired in the Colony.

The Election of 1890 turned upon this question, and of the 24 Members returned to the Legislative Council, 14 were pledged for Responsible Government and 10 against. This majority . . . represents one-sixth of the whole number of Members, and is equal to a majority of about 112 in the British House of Commons.

I concur in the following opinion of Sir C. Mitchell upon the result of the Elections:

'I cannot help regarding it as a fair proof that public opinion in Natal is nearly equally divided on the question. The Constitutional means of giving expression to the views of the Colony have resulted, however, in a decided majority of representatives being returned in favour of

Responsible Government, and it is, therefore, I submit, to be taken as signifying the desire of the Colony, as a Constitutional whole, for that form of Government.'

I may add that Sir C. Mitchell, in private letters, urges Her Majesty's Government to agree to the change, and there is no reason to suppose that the balance of opinion has altered since the Election.

. . . There is force in the argument that as responsible for the internal government of the country, the Ministers must have a voice in Native Affairs, and that to vest independent powers in the Governor as Supreme Chief—as for instance the power of dividing or removing Tribes, or of calling out armed men for warlike service—would be inconsistent with that form of Government. This policy of transferring Native Affairs generally to the Colonial Government has been carried out both in the Cape and New Zealand.

The effect of the Clause (8) will be, that although in certain cases something which the Governor thinks of importance may be left undone because the Executive Council refuse to advise it, the Governor will not be compelled to take any action, as Supreme Chief, of which he disapproves. Moreover by the Royal Instructions he is empowered to disregard the advice of his Executive Council; and further by the Bill itself, Clause 10, and by the Royal Instructions he is bound to reserve any Bill 'whereby persons, not of European birth or descent, may be subjected or made liable to any disabilities or restrictions to which persons of European birth or descent are not also subjected or liable' . . .

. . . I think, therefore, that this compromise may be accepted, as while it gives to the responsible Ministers a voice in Native Affairs, there is sufficient security against harsh measures being adopted. . . .

Signed,
K.[7] 23 October, 1891

Cab. 37/30/37

8   The South African situation

The London Convention of 1884 defined the relationship which in theory prevailed between the British and Transvaal Governments in 1899. Differences between the two governments were widened by the Jameson raid of 1895-6, and reached the point of war in October 1899. This memorandum by the Secretary of State for the Colonies, Joseph Chamberlain, just over a month

[7] The Secretary of State for the Colonies, Lord Knutsford.

before the Boer ultimatum to the British Government and the outbreak of
war sets out his views on relations between the two countries.

Colonial Office memorandum, 6 September 1899
Our relations with the Transvaal have now entered upon a critical
stage. We have practically exhausted our efforts on the lines hitherto
followed, and it is necessary that the Cabinet should come to a decision
as to the policy to be henceforth followed.

. . . What is now at stake is the position of Great Britain in South
Africa—and with it the estimate formed of our power and influence in
our Colonies and throughout the world.

The importance of the present issue is due to the exceptional character of our position in South Africa.

The population at the present time of British and Dutch South Africa
is (very roughly) estimated at 4,000,000, of which 430,000 are of
British origin, 410,000 are Dutch, and the remaining 3,160,000 natives.
The contest for supremacy is between the Dutch and the English—the
natives are interested spectators, with a preference for the English as
their masters, but ready to take the side of the strongest.

The present attitude of the Dutch both in our own Colonies and in
the Orange Free State, illustrates the special difficulty with which we
are confronted in dealing with racial sentiment.

In neither case have they the slightest material grievances. We have
had no dispute of any kind with the Orange Free State for nearly a
generation. To the Dutch in our own Colonies we have given equal
rights and privileges with those of our own nationality—we have
allowed political agitations to continue to the verge of treason—we
have seen, without objection, a Dutch minority returning a majority of
Members to the Cape Legislature and thus securing a Ministry wedded
to Dutch interests.

Yet in spite of all this we are to-day in doubt whether the Orange
Free State and a considerable proportion of our Dutch fellow-subjects
will not make common cause with our enemies, and we know as a fact
that their sympathies will be with them even if their fears and self-
interest prevent them from giving material aid.

The reason for this lies wholly in the existence of the Transvaal
Republic and in the policy which has been pursued by the Oligarchy at
Pretoria.

The Dutch in South Africa desire, if it be possible, to get rid altogether of the connection with Great Britain, which to them is not a
motherland, and to substitute a United States of South Africa which,

they hope, would be mainly under Dutch influence. This idea has always been present in their minds, and has frequently been publicly avowed by indiscreet advocates of their cause. Indeed, I am not certain that Mr. Rhodes did not play up to this ideal when he talked of 'the elimination of the Imperial factor' some years before the Raid. But it would probably have died out as a hopeless impossibility but for the evidence of successful resistance to British supremacy by the South African Republic. The existence of a pure Dutch Republic flouting, and flouting successfully, British control and interference, is answerable for all the racial animosities which have become so formidable a factor in the South African situation.

The suspense and tension of the last few years, and especially of the last few months, has immensely increased the bitterness of feeling which has always existed more or less since 1881. Every one, natives included, sees that issue has been joined, and that it depends upon the action of the British Government now whether the supremacy, which we have claimed so long and so seldom exerted, is to be finally established and recognized or for ever abandoned.

. . . During the whole period which has elapsed since the Convention of Pretoria, we have had constant complaints to make against the action of the South African Republic, but we have never received any satisfactory redress except in the cases in which an ultimatum has been sent accompanied by a display of force.

Meanwhile, the Transvaal and the Orange Free State have been constantly increasing their military preparations, so that, while an expedition of 3,000 men was sufficient in 1884 to secure the fulfilment of their obligations, it is now considered that 50,000 men are required to enforce our claims at the present time. The result is that unless a complete change of policy is secured we shall have to maintain permanently in South Africa a very large garrison, at a great expense to the British taxpayer, and involving the utter disorganization of our military system. . . .

J. C.[8] 6 September, 1899   Cab. 37/50/70

9 The economic and political state of South Africa, 1905

The Treaty of Vereeniging of 1902 promised the Transvaal and Orange River Colony internal self-government. The British Government conceded

[8] The Secretary of State for the Colonies, Joseph Chamberlain.

this form of government to the Transvaal in December, 1906, and the Orange River Colony in June, 1907.

The Earl of Selborne was High Commissioner, the Earl of Elgin Secretary of State for the Colonies.

Memorandum by the Earl of Selborne, addressed to the Earl of Elgin

You may wish to have a general report as to the state of South Africa economically and politically. This I will endeavour to give in as few words as possible.

Ever since the war South Africa has been going through a severe period of depression, enhanced by three years of unprecedented drought, and in the Transvaal by the ravages of the Rhodesian redwater fever, the worst form of cattle disease which South Africa has yet experienced. Cape Colony and Natal are in serious financial difficulties, and are still at that point where the Governments have the greatest difficulty in balancing their Budgets. The Orange River Colony, by skilful and economical administration, has always balanced its Budget, and has a little money in hand. This season promises to be a far better one than the last three, and therefore, from the agricultural point of view, the prospect is generally brighter. You must remember that the farmers in the Transvaal and in the Orange River Colony are, speaking generally, in a state of extreme poverty. They lost everything during the war, and drought and locusts and cattle disease in the Transvaal have delayed the commencement of the process of recovery. Nevertheless, there has been a recovery, but the farmers are still very poor, and the country is, speaking broadly, still unstocked.

. . . Industrially, there is no sign of the return of prosperity in any of the Colonies except the Transvaal. Here, entirely owing to the increased output of the mines, the revenue and the railway receipts are steadily rising, as also is the employment of labour, white and coloured, outside the mines; while on the mines themselves, of course, the increase of employment, both to whites and coloured has been very great. Therefore, judged by ordinary standards, the Transvaal is entering on a period of greater prosperity. But, nevertheless, it is true that there is still great depression among men of business and trade of all kinds. . . .

Politically, the situation is as follows:

The party at present in power in Cape Colony are staunch and loyal to the British connexion, but they hold power by precarious tenure, and may easily be replaced by the Bond. A British Government at Cape Colony makes things much easier for the Transvaal. A Bond

Government might cause us a great deal of trouble. Natal is entirely British and absolutely loyal. The Orange River Colony is practically entirely Boer, but Boers of a higher type, both in character and in education, than those to be found in the Transvaal. In Cape Colony the Boers, whatever their private opinions may be, implicitly obey the instructions of the Bond leaders, Mr. Hofmeyr and Mr. Malan. In the Transvaal the Boers similarly implicitly obey the instructions of the Central Committee of Het Volk, consisting of Generals Botha and De la Rey, Messrs. Smuts, Esselen, and Wolmarans, Schalk Burger, and Beyers. For the attitude of the Boers generally in Cape Colony I would refer you to Sir Walter Hely Hutchinson. About the Bond leaders I will speak presently. As regards the Boers generally in the Transvaal and in the Orange River Colony, I say without hesitation that they have had a sickener of war, and nothing but a most extraordinary opportunity of regaining their independence would ever induce them to take up arms again. . . .

At present in the Orange River Colony there is no organization corresponding with the Bond in Cape Colony or with Het Volk in the Transvaal, but Messrs. Hertzog, Fischer, Ex-President Steyn, and General de Wit, are endeavouring to form one, and they will probably succeed. The leaders of these three organizations will work in co-operation, and the man who will sway the whole is Mr. Hofmeyr at the Cape. The whole Boer people, in fact, from the Cape to the Zambesi, will be directed by a small band of educated men who, with the exception of the fighting generals Botha, De la Rey, and De Wet, are not farmers, but professional men living in towns, and educated in Europe. Now, these men had an ideal before the war, and they have got it still, and it is an ideal which is never absent from their thoughts, and which governs all their policy. It is to form a United Republic of South Africa, to which British colonials will be gladly admitted, but only on condition that it is a Republic with its own flag, and that the predominant influence is Boer, not British. Now, there is nothing dishonourable in this ideal, quite the contrary; but it is absolutely antagonistic to the British ideal, and therefore there can be no compromise with it. What is dishonourable is the trickery and falsehood with which the propagation of this ideal is too often accompanied. . . . But these men are at the present moment thinking no more of an armed rising than are the farmers, unless such an extraordinary opportunity presented itself as one can scarcely imagine. No; their policy at the present moment is exactly what mine would be in similar circumstances—that is, to acquire power under a system of full Responsible Government at the first opportunity,

F

and then to use it remorselessly to diminish British influence in every way, to diminish the number of British in the country, to oust British officials in every Department for Boer officials, to replace the British officers and men in the South African Constabulary by Boer officers and men, to fill the staff on the railways and everywhere else with Boers. They would then feel secure of being able to effect their purpose whenever an opportunity arose . . .

14 December, 1905   Cab. 37/81/179

10   The Union of South Africa

A convention of delegates from the Cape, Natal, Transvaal and the Orange River Colony which met at Durban in 1908 drafted a bill providing a constitution in the form of a union of South Africa. A schedule appended to the bill set out future constitutional arrangements for Basutoland, Swaziland, and the Bechuanaland protectorate.

(a) *Colonial Office memorandum, March 1909*

DRAFT SOUTH AFRICAN CONSTITUTION BILL
(GENERAL PROVISIONS)

A despatch from Lord Selborne is appended, commenting on certain clauses of the draft South African Constitution Bill as it emerged from the South African Convention. His comments on the Schedule dealing with the Protectorates are being circulated with a separate Memorandum.

In this case, as in that of the Australian Commonwealth Act of 1901, His Majesty's Government will doubtless desire to accept and obtain the approval of Parliament for the Bill as finally submitted to them, unless alteration in any particular is judged necessary in Imperial interests. It will be remembered that the draft Bill has yet to be approved by the South African Parliaments, and that it will eventually be brought over, as approved, by a delegation. His Majesty's Government will have the opportunity of discussing any points which may arise with the delegation, but this does not, of course, preclude prior communication through the High Commissioner on any points of difficulty.

Of the points raised by Lord Selborne it does not appear necessary to consider any amendment of clause 65 (power of disallowance) or clause 106 (Appeals). Experience indicates that one year is an ample time in which to consider whether the power of disallowance should be exercised, and the provisions as to appeals generally follow the Australian model, and are in accordance with the resolution of the Colonial Conference of 1907 on the subject. . . .

. . . The effect of clause 153 is that any part of the Constitution can be altered by a Parliamentary majority (subject, of course, to the power of disallowance by His Majesty), except the clause as to appeals (106) and the Protectorates' Schedule (alterations to be reserved for signification of His Majesty's pleasure), and clauses 32–33 (distribution of Members of the Assembly), clause 35 (protection of Cape coloured voters), and clause 138 (equality of Dutch and English languages), alteration of which must be approved by both Houses of Parliament sitting together and approved by a two-thirds vote. The Constitution is thus more easily alterable than either the Canadian (which requires Imperial legislation) or the Australian (which requires a referendum), and it may be argued that in view of this fact there should be a provision, as there is in the recent Transvaal and Orange River Colony Constitutions, providing for reservation of all laws amending the Constitution. It may be maintained that reservation gives time for reflection, and avoids the necessity for having recourse to the extreme step of disallowance. On the other side it must be stated that general reservation of all Bills amending the Constitution is quite unnecessary, and is, indeed, very inconvenient. It will be remembered that in 1907 an Imperial Act was actually passed to get rid of such general reservation in the case of the Australian States' Constitutions. The only question which will probably be raised in Parliament is the absence of reservation of Bills affecting coloured persons such as is contained in the Transvaal and Orange River Colony Letters Patent and Natal Royal Instructions. The answer will be that there will be under the Union over 20,000 coloured voters in Cape Colony, whose influence will have effect throughout the Union. A further consideration is that reservation implies continuance of control by His Majesty's Government. Continuance of control implies continuance of Parliamentary activity here in South African affairs, and continuance of pressure on His Majesty's Government to intervene, for example, on behalf of the coloured or native population. When His Majesty's Government are dealing with a Union Government such intervention will be more dangerous than it is now, and success will be far more difficult of attainment. Intervention in an extreme case might, of course, be inevitable, but in such a case it is always possible to instruct the Governor-General to reserve the particular enactment which is in question.

C.O., March 1909   Cab. 37/98/52

(b) *Letter from the National Council of Basutoland to the High Commisioner for South Africa, 2 May 1909*

National Council Buildings
Maseru, May 2nd, 1909

To His Excellency the Right Honourable
    The Earl of Selborne G.C.M.G., P.C.,
        His Majesty's High Commissioner for South Africa.
Your Excellency,
    During your Lordship's last visit to Basutoland, your Lordship told us that the white inhabitants of South Africa have agreed upon uniting and forming one South African Government. Your Lordship told us that Basutoland must also be prepared to join this Union sooner or later. His Majesty the King also spoke as your Lordship has done, to our representatives, who went to England. The National Council beg to forward to Your Excellency the reply, the opinion and the wishes of the Basutoland Nation with reference to the provisions of the Schedule to the Draft Act of the Constitution.
    What the Basuto wish for is to remain under the direct Government of His Majesty the King only, as they are to-day. If they have to join, the Paramount Chief, Chiefs and the National Council beg to forward to Your Excellency with humbleness the conditions they desire His Majesty King Edward VII. to provide for them in writing, before the Schedule to the Draft Act is approved of by His Majesty. . . .

C.O. 417/468

(c) *Letter from the Paramount Chief and Chiefs of Basutoland to the King, 3 May 1909*
Enclosure in H. C.'s Despatch⎤
No 296 of 10/5/1909   ⎦

National Council Buildings,
Maseru, May 3rd, 1909

To His Excellency
    The Right Honourable
        The Earl of Selborne, G.C.M.G., P.C.,
            His Majesty's High Commissioner
                for South Africa.
YOUR EXCELLENCY
    With respect and humility we beg Your Excellency to forward the thanks of the Paramount Chief, Chiefs and the Nation of Basutoland to His Majesty the King for the promise His Majesty has made for the

Basuto that the land and the National Council shall be preserved for the Basuto; and that brandy will be prohibited in this country. . . .

C.O. 417/468

[The letter is signed by the Paramount Chief Letsie and Chiefs]

11 A proposed visit to South Africa by the King

Memorandum by the Secretary of State for the Colonies, 10 December 1913
I think my colleagues ought to see the following letters from Lord Gladstone[9] and General Botha,[10] though I have not changed my view that it is impossible for the King to visit one Dominion without visiting all, and that the absence of the Sovereign from this country for so long a time and at so great a distance as would be entailed by a visit to Australia and New Zealand is highly undesirable. The date suggested by General Botha for a visit by the King to South Africa is September 1915, a date which might easily coincide with a General Election in this country and subsequent developments which would necessitate the presence of the Sovereign.

L. H.

December 10, 1913

Lord Gladstone to Mr. L. Harcourt

Government House, Pretoria,

My dear Harcourt,   November 20, 1913.
    . . . I have received the enclosed letter from the Prime Minister. He returns to his previous petition that the King should visit South Africa. . . . Recent events and developments have only strengthened my conviction that if constitutional views allow it, a visit by His Majesty would be of immense benefit to South Africa. The Prime Minister has admirably maintained the Imperial idea. He has reasoned or constrained his people into acceptance of his position. So far as he then and his party are concerned, the presence of the King would greatly strengthen his hands and consolidate the best kind of Imperial feeling in his party.
    Hertzog and his people on the other hand, without being disloyal, do their utmost to put Imperialism in the background, and take every opportunity of extolling the Afrikander independent spirit at the expense of the Prime Minister, and in a tone derogatory to the Empire.

---

    [9] Governor-General.   [10] Prime Minister of the Union of South Africa.

I am convinced that the personal presence of the King would soften and weaken the anti-Imperial tendencies of this undoubtedly large and important section of the community.

I believe the Labour Party as a whole to be thoroughly loyal to the King. But the revolutionary elements are getting their chance. The King's presence would renew and greatly strengthen all the best elements in a growing and rather formidable party.

South African parties for various reasons are in a rut. Inspiration and consolidation by the predominant and accepted personality of the King would lift everyone up and teach unity for great objects removed far above the somewhat sordid views, interests, and personal, or party, squabbles, which I regret to say prevent a high standard in political thought and action. If only, at the present moment, we could have a few fine phrases from the King, I am certain they would be wonderfully effective in educating and lifting South African opinion on the whole of the British Indian question.

If constitutional reasons are prohibitive at a given time there is nothing more to be said. But I do firmly think that the issues here in this new, raw country are of an importance to justify such risks as there may be from jealousies—thoroughly patriotic be it remembered—in other Dominions.

Here we are far more out of touch with the Empire in its really great sense than perhaps any important part of it elsewhere. The iron is hot, and it wants moulding and hammering.

Over and above all this I cannot exaggerate the excellent effect on the natives. Their loyalty and goodwill mean everything to South Africa.

Would not the other Dominions understand all this, and so be satisfied on hopes and expectations without promises? I am sure you and your colleagues will carefully weigh these considerations.

Yours sincerely,

GLADSTONE

ENCLOSURE

General Botha to Lord Gladstone
(Confidential.)   *Prime Minister's Office, Pretoria,*
Dear Lord Gladstone,   *November 12, 1913.*

I have again discussed with my colleagues the question of an invitation to His Majesty the King to visit the Union, and they agree with me that the time has come when I should once more urge that the opening of our Union Buildings would offer a most suitable opportunity for such a visit. I . . . will only emphasize the beneficial results from a visit by His Majesty, and that it would be the means of tying closer the bonds which it is our strong desire to see strengthened.

We hope, therefore, that you may be good enough to . . . support this respectful appeal in the strongest manner possible, in order to ascertain whether there is any prospect of a formal invitation to His Majesty to visit the Union receiving favourable consideration.

. . . the conviction of the enormous good which would ensue, and the strong hope that we may be so honoured which exists amongst all classes of our population, and which has been much encouraged by rumours of a contemplated Royal visit to other Dominions, emboldens us to make this humble appeal. . . .

Louis Botha.
Cab. 37/117/89

12   Renewal of the charter of the British South Africa Company

The Crown granted a charter to the British South Africa Company in 1889 to secure Matabeleland and Mashonaland, and the regions north of the Zambesi river including Barotseland. The company would block Transvaal expansion north into Matabeleland and Mashonaland. It hoped to find and develop mineral wealth in the north. It would keep open for development by Great Britain the region north of the Zambesi river.

Extract from a report by the Prime Minister, H. Asquith, to King George V on a Cabinet discussion
. . . (9) Charter of British South Africa Company
The first 25 years of the Charter expire on the 29th October next, and it must then be either cancelled or renewed for 10 years. There are in Rhodesia about 25,000 whites, and 1,750,000 coloured people, and it appeared to the Cabinet that the direct assumption of the Government by the Crown is, for the time, unadvisable. They adopted Mr. Harcourt's proposal to renew the Charter for 10 years, reserving power (as the Company agree) at any time within the 10 years to grant responsible Government.

22 September 1914   Cab. 41/35/46

13 General Botha's views

Report by the Governor-General of South Africa, 19 November 1915

I circulate to my colleagues this interesting account by Lord Buxton[11] of conversations with General Botha.

A. B. L.[12]

December 20, 1915

Cape Town, Friday, November 19, 1915

Botha came to see me after the House was up, and I had a long talk with him on various matters . . .

. . . he was not altogether happy about the political position; and he felt that the Nationalists were going to carry on an active campaign founded on a continuation of misrepresentation, personal abuse, and racial feeling.

However, he had no fears (he expressed this more than once) of any outbreak, but only of general unrest. But the fact that something like 77,000 of the Dutch electors had voted Nationalist obviously created a serious and anxious political position.

He agreed that it would be inexpedient for Smuts to go to German East Africa, at all events at present; this coinciding with Smuts' own view.

He said that he thought it would be an expedient thing, from the point of view of military education, if, when matters settle down here, Smuts could pay a visit to Europe, and visit the front there.

Caucus.—I asked him how he got on with his Caucus. On the whole he was satisfied with the position. He said that unfortunately some of his new members, not being accustomed to Parliamentary elections, had somewhat pledged themselves against any contribution towards the Contingent. But he thought he would be able to get over this difficulty, and he had put it to them very strongly that they must consider the feelings of the British, who represented nearly half the population. He was confident that, though some of them might be somewhat unwilling, he would lose no votes.

He told them that if he quarrelled with the Unionists another election would be necessary—and this they would not like. . . .

---

[11] Governor-General of the Union of South Africa.
[12] Andrew Bonar Law, Secretary of State for the Colonies.

Outlook.—As regards the general outlook, in his view the present acute position was dependent on, and would only continue, as long as the war lasted.

He said, 'When the war is over we shall knock them out,' and that he was sure that on the day when peace (a satisfactory peace) was signed, the difficulties in this country would be over. That until then the Nationalists would do everything to hamper the Government and raise disloyal feeling.

He thought that on the whole his policy was making progress, and that some of the more moderate Nationalists would be inclined to support him. 'We shall go on all right,' he said, 'if we do nothing foolish, and shall knock them out' ('them' being the Nationalists).

He hoped that the Home Government would understand that his policy had been, and continued to be, what he called 'to take advantage of the friendly British tide'.

In his view the Nationalists were 'all against the Flag'. (I rather demurred to this as regards the Cape Nationalists as a whole.)

Visit to England.—I read him the Secretary of State's letter enclosing to me the answer which he had given in reference to the invitation to the Prime Ministers of the other Dominions to pay a visit to England with a view to a full and confidential discussion. Bonar Law advised me that he had not sent an invitation to Botha of the same kind, as he fully realised how impossible it would be for him to get away.

Botha said that of course it would be impossible for him to get away at present, but the time might come when such a visit would be possible.

He said, chaffingly, that if he were the Prime Minister in England he would consider the presence of the Dominion Prime Ministers at a time of great stress and strain such as this as 'a damned nuisance', as they would be certain to be, from his experience, fussing about without being of much practical value!

At the same time he appreciated the invitation. But if he did go over to Europe what he would specially desire, rather than merely to discuss matters in London, would be to go to the front in order to have an opportunity of seeing the war under war conditions. He would have liked to have gone and done this at once if his duty here did not prevent it. But he was quite sure that he could at present do more good to assist the Empire by remaining here to see it through rather than by going to England. . . .

Cab. 37/139/42

14   Report by Lord Buxton of a visit to Rhodesia in 1916

I circulate to the Cabinet an interesting account received from Lord Buxton of his visit to Rhodesia.

A. B. L.

Colonial Office, August 14, 1916

Visit of His Excellency the High Commissioner (Viscount Buxton) to Rhodesia . . . June 1916
This was my first visit to Rhodesia.

. . . *Visit to Khama.*—On the way up we paid a visit to Khama (Paramount Chief of the Bamangwato) at his 'capital' Serowe.

. . . Certainly the variety and beauty of Rhodesia is very marked.

The Settlers.—I had the pleasure of meeting all the leading people (some of whom I knew before), including all the members of the Legislative Council, official and unofficial, excepting two who were away.

I was struck, and so was Lady Buxton, with the high standard of knowledge and intelligence and keenness of the settlers, both men and of women [*sic*], especially at Bulawayo.

They take a real interest in Rhodesia. They are proud of being Rhodesians, in spite of some grumbling and abuse or criticism of 'the Company.' They, for the most part, intend to live and die there—indeed, one meets no small number of the original settlers of twenty to twenty-five years ago who are still living there.

. . . Rhodesia can indeed claim, and with justice, that she has proved her loyalty in the most practical way by taking a full share in the War. It is estimated that no less than forty per cent. (some put the percentage higher) of the adult male whites in Southern Rhodesia are at the front, either in Europe or in East or Central Africa.

Besides those who have gone to the front, a very large proportion of the remainder are members of the various Volunteer and Defence and Cadet Corps; efficient, and ready to take the field if and when it became necessary for the defence of the Territory, or in consequence of native unrest. . . .

. . . The most marked feature of Rhodesia, as far as the white inhabitants are concerned, is that they are typically 'English' (using that word as including the United Kingdom). 'A bit of England,' was a phrase I used in one of my speeches. They are proud of being purely British, and that they form a part of the Empire; and they crave for public recognition of this fact.

Racial Question.—All their habits, tastes, feelings and thoughts are British, and Rhodesia is, as yet, practically untouched by the racial question. The few Dutch settlers are for the most part of the poorer type; and they mostly congregate together and keep themselves to themselves. Dutch expressions, such as 'stoep,' &c., are taboo, and any considerable incursion of Dutch would be popularly resented; though I do not think there is any real antipathy to the Dutch as such. Throughout the Union, on the other hand, the racial question is ever either active or latent. It cannot be ignored; one cannot get away from it; it dominates politics, opinion, and daily life. Tactful handling and time may perhaps gradually reduce its activity and virulence, but it never can wholly disappear.

. . . *Education.*—The schools in Rhodesia, especially in Bulawayo, Salisbury and Umtali, thanks to the educational wishes of the settlers and to the enlightened policy of the Company, are distinctly good, and the attendance is remarkable. We were struck also with the healthy intelligent appearance of the children. . . .

. . . *Relations between Settlers and Chartered Company.*—The relations between the citizens and settlers and the British South Africa Company in Southern Rhodesia are at present, I think, on the whole not unsatisfactory. Matters of dispute and antagonism are of course perpetually arising. I feel sure, however, that the creation of a representative Legislative Council, with now a substantial majority of elected members, has been most advantageous. It has enabled steam to be let off in a constitutional way; while the discussions in the Council, and the personal relations which are brought about between the official and unofficial members, have materially assisted towards better mutual relationship.

Of course the question of finance is at the bottom of most of the difficulties. The settlers press this, that, or the other expenditure, and the Company, being hard up, have to put them off as best they can with refusals or promises. It is, indeed, rather a marvel how the Company have managed to finance Southern Rhodesia all these years. The shareholders, of course, have so far never received a sixpence.

The Local Administration.—The local Administration, as distinct from the London Board of the Company, is held, so it appeared to me, in good esteem by the inhabitants. They are not held responsible for the alleged niggardly or mistaken policy of the Company, and they carry out their duties efficiently and tactfully.

Both Sir Charles Coghlan, who leads the representative members in the Legislative Council, and Colonel Raleigh Grey, who is one of the most prominent and the most independent of them, bore witness publicly in my presence to the good relations which existed between the representative members and the Administration as such. . . .

Position in Northern Rhodesia.—At Livingstone, Northern Rhodesia, the position unfortunately is different. A certain section of the settlers, and especially of the citizens of Livingstone, are on terms of friction not only with the Company, but with the Administrator and with the Administration. As I heard it described, it is rather like 'town' and 'gown' at Oxford or Cambridge, 'gown' being represented by the Administration and civil servants, and 'town' by the so-called commercial element.

. . . the Constitution of Northern Rhodesia is entirely different to that of Southern Rhodesia, for the citizens and settlers have at present no voice whatever in the Administration.

It appears to me that the Company would be well advised if, assuming that the amalgamation of Northern and Southern Rhodesia (which if adopted would in itself give Northern Rhodesia direct representation) is not carried through, they were to agree to some form of representation in the nature of a Council. This might contain three or four elected members, with the official element in the majority. At present, at all events, so the 'agitators' told me, the settlers are not asking for a majority on the proposed Council. . . .

Cab. 37/152/34

X

BRITISH EAST AFRICA
European demands and non-European claims

Between 1880 and 1932 Uganda became a British protectorate, Kenya a British colony and Tanganyika a League of Nations mandate under the British crown. British policy was shaped in the early years largely by strategic and humanitarian considerations, but economic factors became more prominent after the building of the railway in 1901. The presence of Europeans and non-Europeans other than Africans raised complex constitutional problems, but the doctrine of paramountcy of African interests stated in the 1923 White Paper was reaffirmed in subsequent government papers. The British Government denied the Europeans internal self-government.

1 Uganda

(a) *Foreign Office memorandum, 10 September 1892*
I am circulating to the Cabinet the inclosed Memorandum on Uganda by Sir Percy Anderson, head of the African Department in the Foreign Office, and I shall soon have to circulate further papers on the same subject; for the matter is pressing, and will not be able to stand over for the regular autumn Cabinet meetings.

Communication to Uganda from Mombasa takes three months; the Company evacuates Uganda on the 31st December, and, therefore, if action is to be taken, it will have to be taken soon.

R. (Ripon)[1]

Memorandum
South of the East, Central, and West Soudan, which are under the rule of Mahommedan Chiefs, the strongest kingdom is that of Uganda. It is a powerful native State, governed by a King, with Councillors; there is a Court, an army, an intelligent and industrious population. As is usual in Africa, its area varies according to circumstances. It has claimed supremacy over all the regions bordering Victoria Nyanza; it has

[1] The Secretary of State for the Colonies, Lord Ripon.

within our knowledge exercised it, and is believed now to exercise it, over the whole of those surrounding the northern half of that lake.

For fifteen years Christian missionaries have been at work in it. Their success has been exceptional. The Church Missionary Society opened the ground. Their first party reached Rubaga on the 30th June, 1877; French Roman Catholic priests followed, arriving on the 23rd February, 1879. The conversion of the then reigning King by the former led to the adhesion of his subjects in large numbers. There have been many vicissitudes, including the murder of Bishop Hannington in 1885, but the missionaries have held their own; numerically the Roman Catholics preponderate. Before the advent of the missionaries the Arab and Swahili slave-dealers were all-powerful; they have fought hard to retain their position, and have had their triumphs, marked by massacres of Christians and the expulsion of missionaries. They are at present waiting their opportunity in the neighbouring country of Unyoro. They have been recently defeated by Captain Lugard, but will not lightly relinquish their hope of re-establishing themselves in the best slave-raiding region of Central Africa. They are favoured by the dissensions between the two sections of Christians, who have formed themselves into opposing political factions, how far encouraged by the missionaries we have hardly sufficient material for deciding.

The position of Uganda may be thus briefly summarized. When visited by Speke and Grant in 1862, and by Stanley in 1875, it was a wholly barbarous State, but nevertheless a State. Its Government, firm and far-reaching, had the vices of barbarism fostered for selfish purposes by the Arabs. It revelled in wars, conquests, wholesale depopulations, slave-making, and slave-trading. European influences have checked these vices, and with peace the country will be civilized, but if the influences are removed it will at once relapse. Meanwhile, the civilizing process is retarded by the conflicts among the whites. Whatever may be its future, it must be an important factor in the anti-slavery struggle. Its resources would be invaluable to the slave-traders; on the other hand, it is the only native State that can resist Arabs of the type found in the Upper Basin of the Congo.

Its connection with European political combinations dates from 1885. The assumption by Germany on the 17th February, 1885, of a Protectorate in East Africa, and the restriction of the power of the Sultan of Zanzibar to a strip of territory on the coast as the result of a Delimitation Commission, and an Agreement between England, Germany, and France, alarmed the King as to his independence, and deprived the whites of such protection as they derived from the indirect influence of the Sultan. The immediate results were the death of Bishop Hannington in 1885 at the instigation of the King of Uganda, and the temporary restoration of the power of the Arabs. Apprehension was expressed by religious and trading bodies in England as to the aims of Germany, and not without reason. German agents were annexing all that was valuable. Their activity was checked by the Anglo-German Agreement of 1886, by which a boundary was drawn. The guiding principle of this demarcation was a partition of the caravan routes to Uganda; the route reaching the coast at Mombasa was placed on the English, that terminating at Pangani on the German, side. Both parties recognized the importance of Uganda as a trade centre. The line was not carried beyond the eastern shore of Victoria Nyanza, consequently did not deal with the main portion of Uganda, which was, however, indirectly severed from German influence by the subsequent 'Hinterland' understanding.

A field for English commercial enterprise having been secured, the British East Africa Company was formed to develop the territory. The Company obtained a Concession from the Sultan of his mainland strip in 1887, and a Charter from the Crown in 1888. There is no question that the objects of the founders of this Company were primarily humanitarian, though it was hoped that it might pay its way. The preamble of the Charter correctly defined its objects. . . .

Cautious advisers, such as Sir John Kirk, recommended the development of the countries near the coast, and a gradual advance into the interior.

The Company's hand was forced by the active hostility of the German Colonization Society, whose object was to throttle English enterprise. I obtained at Berlin in 1890 proof of the ambitious schemes of the Society. The Company was to be hemmed in on all sides. The German programme was to annex the territory to the north between the Tana and the Juba, Uganda, and the region between the lake and the Congo State, and to sweep round from the Upper Nile, north of the Congo State, to the Cameroons. There was more in it which need not be referred to.

Dr. Peters was dispatched by the Society to carry out the programme, and did so with energy. He ascended the Tana, and worked round to Uganda, whence he re-entered the German sphere, where he learned that his journey was valueless, owing to the conclusion of the Berlin Agreement of 1st July, 1890. Had these schemes, or a portion of them, been carried out, English enterprise must have been confined to the Zanzibar coast and its immediate neighbourhood.

If there had been no pressure from Germany, and if Uganda had been friendly and independent, the Company might have adhered to its original policy; but the course of events above sketched forced it to advance in order to prevent the King from becoming actively hostile to the British and to protect the missionaries. In the meanwhile, the Directors had, in the previous April, with a view to the negotiations with Germany, communicated to Her Majesty's Government the steps they were about to take to secure control over Uganda, and strongly urged the necessity for a clear understanding as to the settled line of delimitation of the German and British spheres of influence to the west of the Victoria Nyanza Lake, so as to insure its possession. Mr. Jackson, as leader of a caravan, had been sent to the lake with orders not to interfere in Uganda. The appearance on the scene of Dr. Peters, with the German flag, left him no alternative. He entered Uganda in May 1890. He has, however, been censured by the missionaries for risking, as they allege, the lives of the Protestants by his delay: in reply he points to his instructions. He did not conclude a Treaty, but Captain Lugard, who followed him in September of the same year, and found the position of the missionaries and their followers at the mercy of a capricious and sanguinary King, surrounded by perils, succeeded in so doing on the 26th December, 1890. The country was thus taken under the Company's control.

It soon became obvious to the Directors that the expenditure was beyond their resources. It was necessary to maintain a small military force, and to keep it supplied from the coast by means of caravans. The outlay was estimated by Sir William Mackinnon at 40,000*l.* a-year. He made in this estimate provision for the cost of a heavy caravan service, and it is thought in some quarters that his figure is too high, especially if peace is restored, but a much lower figure would considerably exceed the revenue from the net receipts from the customs, which are esti-mated at about 8,000*l.* a-year.

The railway project was then brought forward. It was urged that, with communication by rail, the expense of holding Uganda would be trifling. But the construction of the railway was impossible for the Company unaided. An appeal was made to Government; it was con-tended that the civilization of Uganda, and consequent extinction of the Slave Trade in a vast region, would be a reasonable and effective con-tribution to the work which Great Britain had undertaken to perform at Brussels, and that the expenditure would be to a great extent met by savings on cruizers. The project was supported in many quarters. The following bodies have memorialized the Government in favour of it:

the Leith, Dewsbury, Birmingham, Bristol, Edinburgh, Blackburn, Leeds, Birmingham, Aberdeen, Nottingham, and Wakefield Chambers of Commerce; Manchester Merchants; and the Anti-Slavery Society. The scheme was favourably entertained, subject to the result of surveys. If they proved that the construction was feasible, it was intended to propose a Government guarantee for the interest on the requisite capital, that is to say, 2 per cent. per annum on a paid-up capital not exceeding 1,250,000*l*.

Meanwhile, the immediate pressure on the Company's funds was relieved through the subscription of 25,000*l*. in October 1891 by the Church Missionary Society and some private persons for the maintenance of the Uganda control. Captain Lugard was told that he should remain till the end of the present year, by which time it was hoped that Government support for the railway project might be secured. With such support assured, the Directors felt that they would be justified in holding on, as they would have reasonable ground for hoping ultimately to recoup their immediate losses. Unavoidable delays, however, occurred. There was obviously no certainty, and on the 16th May last Captain Lugard was positively ordered to withdraw at the end of the present year. He arrived at Mombasa on the 1st instant. Captain Williams, R.A., remains in command in Uganda.

The present position, then, is this. At the end of the year the Company will withdraw, as to stay unaided would be ruin. Uganda will be left uncontrolled. The surveys for the railway have given more favourable results than were anticipated. The apprehensions as to the difficulty of passing through the broken country between the Masai plains and the lake have not been justified. Captain Macdonald finds an easy route up to this barrier, a practicable line through it, and a good port on the lake. The length of the line is about 700 miles, and the estimated cost 2,500,000*l*. Captain Macdonald has been to Uganda, and is expected at Mombasa at the end of September.

It is difficult to forecast the result of withdrawal. The Company will find it useless to stop, in their retreat, short of the advanced posts east of the Masai country, *e.g.*, Dagoreti or Machakos. Uganda, barely recovered from an internecine struggle, can hardly fail to be in a dangerous state. All those who know the country have grave apprehensions. They see the possibility of the return [of] the slave-traders, massacres of missionaries and of their flocks, the resumption of the old system of wars and depopulation of the neighbouring countries. Their fears may be exaggerated; they cannot be groundless.

Bishop Tucker has said that under no circumstances will the

missionaries leave their posts, whatever may be their fate. Writing
to Mr. Portal on the 16th June, he said—

'It may be assumed as an *absolute certainty* that not one of our missionaries will think of retirement on the withdrawal of the Company, and
I am happy to think that when that moment comes I shall have an
opportunity of sharing whatever fate may befall them. To hold our
ground is our plain simple duty, nothing more, and with God's help
we intend to do it.'

Including the Bishop, it is understood that those of the Church
Missionary Society, now in Uganda and on their way there, number
fourteen.* The number of the Roman Catholic missionaries is unknown.

* [A footnote in the original giving their names has been omitted.]

Experienced officers are unanimous in saying that it would be
difficult and expensive to recover the lost position, as the devastation of
the country westward of the foodless Masai country would deprive an
advancing force of the supplies on which it must depend.

Great Britain cannot, if the control is withdrawn, count upon
retaining rights over Uganda. Germany and Italy are debarred from
taking it by their Agreements dated respectively the 1st July, 1890, and
the 24th March, 1891. Germany has, however, posts on the southern
half of the lake, and there are conceivable circumstances under which
humanity might almost compel her intervention. Captain Lugard may,
since the late fighting, have concluded a Treaty debarring the King
from placing himself under another Power, but there may be conditions which, if unfulfilled, would release him from his obligations.
This he will be able to explain; but native Treaties are not uncommonly
disregarded, and there are no international Agreements binding any
Power except Germany and Italy.

In case of withdrawal there is not only Uganda to be considered,
but also the Upper Nile. At present, by the Anglo-German Agreement,
the western watershed of the Upper Nile is placed within the British
sphere. If the occupation of Uganda were continued the regions of that
basin would be brought, by Treaties and otherwise, under British
influence: Major Wingate, of the Intelligence Department, who speaks
as a close observer, gives it as his opinion that the reconquest of Equa-
toria by an European Power holding Uganda would be an easy matter.
Captain Lugard has concluded Treaties and established a line of forts in
a portion of the watershed beyond the limits of Uganda; these would,
on evacuation, be withdrawn. The Congo State and France covet the
watershed. The King of the Belgians has already sent an expedition

into it, and has been warned off by us; if we retire he will probably remain, unless, as is not improbable, the French, who, having advanced close to the watershed, are already at issue with the King as to his right to extend his frontier, push him back and advance themselves into the unoccupied territory. They might do this at once; they might hold their hand at present, and wait for their succession as contingent heirs to the Congo State; but it is necessary to indicate, as a question to be considered, that it is almost certain that if England withdraws her claim to the Upper Nile watershed, one or other of the two Powers will at once replace her, and that we must face the contingency of the Nile Basin, in its upper waters, and the Equatorial Provinces, being brought under French rule. The King of the Belgians has said openly, in his recent communications with Sir Edmund Monson, that if England retires, he will have to make the best terms he can with France, as to whose designs on the Nile he entertains no doubt.

I think I should also indicate, as a question for consideration, the effect which might be produced upon other Powers, especially the parties to the Brussels Act, and those having subjects in the British sphere, if Great Britain were to withdraw from all responsibility in connection with the sphere without providing for the transfer of her responsibilities to another Power.

I believe that the material difficulties as regards the occupation of Uganda are not great. . . .

Calculations as to how far Uganda and the neighbouring territories, if peaceful and well governed, would at present pay the cost of administration must be conjectural; they would certainly contribute something, possibly a sensible proportion. Captain Lugard holds that the Upper Lake districts, including the Salt Lake, would give 'a very substantial return'. The Directors of the Company have no apprehension on this account if, in one form or another, the difficulty of the expenditure on communications can be solved.

H. PERCY ANDERSON

Foreign Office,
September 10, 1892

Cab. 37/31/22

(b) *Despatch from the Commissioner to Uganda, Sir G. Portal, to Lord Rosebery, 14 September 1892 (Received October 1)*
(Private.)
Dear Lord Rosebery,   *Mombasa, September 14, 1892*
    I arrived here yesterday, and have had some long conversations with

Captain Lugard, with some Egyptians who have just come down from Uganda, and with a missionary who has also just arrived from thence by a different road. The result of these conversations has left such a strong impression on my mind, that I venture to trouble you with this line on the subject.

All these people are unanimously of opinion that the withdrawal of the English officers and the Company's forces from Uganda will be the signal for an immediate outbreak of war, which must *inevitably* result in a massacre of Christians such as the history of this century cannot show. There is no hope whatever of Catholics and Protestants combining for their own defence; and, separately, they have not the smallest chance against the Mahommedans and 'heathen' combined.

Moreover, it is inevitable that such a withdrawal, following closely on the pledges and promises of protection and Treaties given by the Company to the various Chiefs, will have the effect of utterly destroying the respect in which the English name is now held in the interior, and will make any extension of influence impossible except by force of arms.

I hope you will see Lugard, who is very strong on the subject. Under a Government administration, if strong enough, Uganda could probably be made self-supporting in a few years.

It must be remembered that messengers sent full speed even *now* would be only *just* in time to stop the withdrawal of the troops from Uganda.

Believe me, &c.

(Signed)   G. H. PORTAL[2]

Cab. 37/31/30

(c) *Foreign Office memorandum for the Cabinet, 16 September 1892*
A decision with regard to Uganda cannot be long delayed, for the Company evacuates Uganda by the 31st of December, 1892.

In order to arrive before the evacuation is begun, counter-instructions should leave Mombasa not later than the 1st of October.

The issues before the Government reduced to their barest shape are these—

1. Whether to allow Uganda to pass out of our hands altogether, by simply remaining passive spectators of evacuation; or

2. In some way or another to prevent this abandonment. This determination would of course imply expenditure of, I trust, a moderate kind.

[2] Consul-General at Zanzibar, Commissioner to Uganda in 1892.

If the first course be decided upon, there is no more to be said. But on every ground, both of principle and expediency, I should deprecate any such decision.

I do not admit, however, that the Company are entitled to cast the slightest responsibility on the Government, or at any rate on this Government. The Company urged the late Government to obtain Uganda for them. Uganda has turned out too costly a possession for them, and they give it up. Had it been a profitable one, the Government would have received no benefit. And the most regrettable phase of this business is this, that the Company gave orders a year ago to evacuate Uganda, but on 26,000*l.* being raised (of which Sir W. Mackinnon contributed 10,000*l.*) the evacuation was postponed in order to give time for reflection. Unfortunately, the money and time are spent, without reflection, and there does not appear to be anything gained, anything proposed, anything thought out. In truth, while the enterprise is creditable to the philanthropy and munificence of Sir W. Mackinnon, it seems to reflect but little lustre on any one except the Englishmen, who, like Lugard and Williams, and in a minor degree Bagge and De Winton, have pushed and sustained it on the spot.

. . . Uganda has become a question of Imperial policy.

In the first place, there is the question of the Nile. At present we are the only civilized nation that has acess to the Nile, and if only in view of the vital interest of the Nile to Egypt, and the peril to Egypt of any diversion of its stream, it is extremely important that we should remain so. But other nations are anxious to obtain a footing on it. The Congo State is asking for the cession of a territory which will give access to it, which we, in view of the extreme probability, to say no more, of the reversion of the Congo State to France, are unwilling to grant. France herself is making for the Nile from the west by trying to force down the boundary-line with the Congo State, so as to give her a route to the Nile, north of the Congo State, from her possessions in the French Congo. Italy on the east is pushing in the same direction. Germany would probably take advantage of our evacuation to step in. Uganda is no doubt outside her sphere of influence. But if we go, and there is a chaos of blood and destruction after our departure, the Germans, whom the Catholics have already thought of summoning, will have a right, in the name of humanity, to come and occupy this long-coveted territory, and to take up the civilizing work that we have abandoned as beyond our strength. I do not say that it is possible permanently to preserve the Nile for Great Britain and for Egypt, but I do say that if we abandon Uganda, we lose at once and by that fact the control of the

Nile. This, however important in point of policy, is, to my mind, the least and the weakest of the considerations which weigh against the evacuation; for [sic].

In the second place, Uganda is the paradise of slave-dealers. Since British influence has prevailed there the Slave Trade has been paralyzed. But the Arabs who live by this Traffic have not moved far off. They are determined, ruthless, and powerful, and they are watching round the State for any chance that may restore to them this happy hunting-ground. If we, who rest on our anti-slavery exertions, perhaps our chief claim to rank among the Agencies of the world that make for good, and certainly our sole claim in the eyes of other nations for dis-interestedness, if we deliberately hand back Uganda to the slave-dealers, we shall be guilty of a grave and perhaps criminal dereliction of duty.

Moreover, to take lower ground, we shall mortally offend that great body of public opinion in this country which holds the uprooting of slavery as an article of religious belief; something broader, more sensi-tive, and more passionate than what is popularly known as the Non-conformist conscience.

Thirdly, there is the certainty of a terrible disaster. The evacuation of Uganda, according to every authority, involves not merely the restora-ation of the Slave Trade, but the massacre of those native Christians who do not fly and of the missionaries who will not fly. These last, Bishop Tucker declares, will not budge; they will die at their posts; it is their duty, it is their privilege. A formidable responsibility, then, is incurred by the Government that has to face this impending tragedy, of which the effect on the public mind would be little, if at all, less than that produced by the fall of Khartoum.

The second and third considerations then to my mind completely eclipse the first. . . .

The question next arises: What is to be done? That seems to me a question which it is useless to discuss until the Cabinet have settled whether *anything* is to be done. Should they decide against the complete evacuation of Uganda it would, I conceive, be necessary for me to frame definite proposals. For the moment, it is sufficient to put aside one proposition. The late Government commenced a survey for a railway from Mombasa to Victoria Nyanza. That survey is now com-pleted, and it is announced that the railroad is quite practicable, and will cost 2,500,000*l.* But, in my opinion, that is not a work of prime necessity as a matter of Imperial policy; and even if it were, I am under the impression that the present Government is largely pledged against

it. Should the Government therefore decide against the evacuation of
Uganda, I shall not propose that the railway shall [this word is deleted
in ink] be commenced.   (Signed) ROSEBERY[3]
Foreign Office,
September 16, 1892

Cab. 37/31/23

(d) *Colonial Office memorandum for the Cabinet, 25 September 1892*
The policy to be pursued in regard to Uganda in the present state of
affairs involves questions of the gravest kind. How grave they are is
clearly shown in the memoranda of Lord Rosebery on the one side and
Sir W. Harcourt on the other. I have before me almost daily at the
Colonial Office proofs of the enormous increase of our responsibilities
involved in Lord Salisbury's African policy; responsibilities of vast
extent, undefined in their character and far reaching in their consequences. From most of them we cannot now draw back.

But the case of Uganda in many respects stands by itself. The country is separated by hundreds of miles from the more southern portions
of the British 'sphere of influence'; it is 800 miles from the coast; and
up to the present time, I believe, our action in regard to it has been confined to giving a Charter to the Imperial British East African Company.
The Company has penetrated into these distant regions and set up a
sort of administration there which has produced results which cannot
be contemplated with much satisfaction, and which have ended in
financial failure. It is admitted that the British Government has no
responsibility towards the Company; Captain Lugard's attempt to fix
responsibility upon us because he happens to be an officer in the Army
is simply ridiculous; and we are, as it seems to me, free to take such
course as we may consider wisest and best for the public interests in the
conjuncture which has arisen.

Lord Rosebery has not told us what he would do. But in the absence
of information on that point I can see no flaw in Sir W. Harcourt's
arguments as to the ultimate consequences of our stepping in to take
over the ruined inheritance of the Company. To my mind there is but
one consideration of weight in favour of the opposite course. Lord
Rosebery says that if the Company abandons Uganda and we do not
take their place 'there is the certainty of a terrible disaster,' that is, of a
massacre of missionaries and Christians of various kinds.

Now, if there is a certainty of such a catastrophe it is enough to make
us pause. Lord Rosebery's endorsement of Captain Lugard's and Sir G.

[3] Secretary of State for Foreign Affairs.

Portal's statements on this subject have made me hesitate greatly as to the judgment which I ought to form upon the course to be followed. Sir W. Harcourt, I think, treats the danger too lightly; that there is some danger I believe, but on the other hand I cannot but regard with considerable suspicion the alarmist prophecies of a man so extravagant in his views and so rash in his purposes as Captain Lugard; while I doubt whether Sir G. Portal's expression of opinion is the result of independent knowledge, and not rather a judgment formed on the statements of Captain Lugard and other officers of the Company, and therefore of no corroborative value.

On the one hand then we have the certainty, for such surely it is, of being involved in the immediate expense and serious difficulties resulting from the attempt to administer a vast territory in Central Africa, and in the ultimate annexation, possibly at no distant day, of the whole of the regions included in the 'sphere' of Captain Lugard's ambition. On the other hand we have prophecies of anarchy and massacre, if we allow the Company to fall to the ground without ourselves occupying their place. The choice is a difficult one. Our information is far from complete. I should earnestly have wished for further knowledge and more complete discussion before I gave a final opinion upon so grave an issue; but if I must say aye or no before the 1st October, I can only give my voice against embarking in an enterprise entailing upon the British Government and People such grave and ill-defined responsibilities of every kind, as would be involved in any attempt to take upon ourselves the work in which the Imperial British East African Company has so utterly failed.

RIPON

25th September, 1892

Cab. 37/31/27

(e) *King Mwanga of Buganda to the Queen 17 June, 1892*
Imperial British East Africa Company to Foreign Office.—(Received October 5.)
Sir,   *2, Pall Mall East, London, October 5, 1892.*
I have the honour to forward herewith, to be laid before the Earl of Rosebery, a letter addressed by King Mwanga, of Uganda, to Her Majesty the Queen, which was intrusted to Captain Lugard for delivery. I also inclose translated copy of the letter. . . .

I am, &c.
(Signed)   ERNEST L. BENTLEY,
Acting Secretary.

Letter from Mwanga to the Queen
(Translation.)   *Buganda, Mengo, June 17, 1892*

To my friend the Queen, our great Sovereign, I and all my Chiefs send you many greetings. I write this letter to thank you. Thank you exceedingly for sending the Representatives of the Company, in order to set my country to rights.

When they reached Buganda, at first I did not like them; I did not think that they could set the country to rights. After we had fought, Captain Lugard wrote me a letter, and invited me and restored me to my kingdom; then he went out and invited the Mahommedans as well, with whom I had been at war, and brought them back, and gave them a part of the country. But now my country is at peace; the agents of the Company have arranged it excellently. Now, I earnestly beseech you to help me; do not recall the Company from my country. I and my Chiefs are under the English flag, as the people of India are under your flag. We desire very, very much that the English should arrange this country. Should you recall these agents of the Company, my friend, my country is sure to be ruined; war is sure to come.

Captain Lugard has now brought to terms these three religions; he has returned to England; he will inform you of the state of affairs in Buganda.

But I want you to send this same Captain Lugard back again to Buganda, that he may finish his work of arranging the country, for he is a man of very great ability, and all the Buganda like him very much. He is gentle, his judgments are just and true; and so I want you to send him back to Buganda.

So, our friend, persevere in helping us, for we are your people.

May God give you blessing and long life. I, Mwanga, King of Buganda, and my great Chiefs. [The names of twelve chiefs follow.]

Cab. 37/32/40

(f) *Foreign Office memorandum, 22 November 1892*

The Chancellor of the Exchequer and I have agreed to submit the following propositions to the Cabinet:—

1. That it is desirable that the evacuation of Uganda by the Company should now proceed without further interference from the Government.

2. That a Commissioner be appointed for the purpose of reporting on the actual state of affairs in Uganda, and the best means of dealing with the country.

3. It would be the duty of Sir G. Portal, whether he go as Commissioner himself or not, to provide a suitable force of Zanzibaris to protect the Commissioner.

R. (Rosebery)

Foreign Office,
November 22, 1892

Cab. 37/32/42

(g) *House of Commons Statement,*[4] *12 April 1894*
. . . After considering the late Sir G. Portal's Report and weighing the consequences of withdrawal from Uganda, on the one hand, and, on the other, of maintaining British interests there, Her Majesty's Government have determined to establish a regular administration, and for that purpose to declare Uganda to be under a British protectorate. The details of the arrangements to be made are under consideration. . . .

Hansard 4s., 1894, 23, 223

2   Somaliland

Foreign Office memorandum, 4 June 1904
In 1884 the British Government established a protectorate over the tribes on the Somali coast extending from Lahadu (Loyi-Ada) to the forty-ninth meridian E. long. The Resident at Aden administered the protectorate as a dependency of the Government of India until 1898, when it was transferred to the Foreign Office. It came under the Colonial Office in 1905.

In 1887 Great Britain and France concluded an agreement to delimit their frontiers in Somaliland.

The policy of His Majesty's Government with regard to the future administration of Somaliland is laid down in the following paragraph of the instructions sent to Colonel Swayne with the assent of the Cabinet on the 19th May:—

'You will clearly understand that the object aimed at is that we should, as soon as possible, be relieved from all military responsibility, except for the coast-line of Somaliland, and that the tribes themselves should be so organized as to enable us to intrust them with the defence of the remoter parts of the Protectorate as well as with the settlement of all inter-tribal questions. Except as an interim arrangement, while the work of organization is in progress, it is not intended that any posts in the interior shall be held by regular troops'. . . .

June 1904   Cab. 37/71/75

4 By the Chancellor of the Exchequer Sir W. G. V. Harcourt.

3 Transfer to the Colonial Office of British Protectorates in East Africa

Foreign Office memorandum, 1905

The West African Protectorate was transferred from the Foreign Office to the Colonial Office seven years ago. The Central African Protectorate was transferred last year.

There now remain three Protectorates under the administration of the Foreign Office, all of them on the east side of Africa and in close connection with one another. These are:

1. East Africa.
2. Uganda.
3. Somaliland.

It has been agreed that the time has come for transferring the administrative business of these Protectorates from the Foreign Office, and it is understood that the Colonial Office are ready to take over East Africa and Uganda from the 1st April next.

There seems, however, to be some hesitation as to accepting the transfer of Somaliland, and the Colonial Office have suggested that it might be handed over to the India Office.

It is only seven years ago that the transfer of the Somaliland Protectorate from the Government of India to the Foreign Office was decided upon on the ground that, in view of our relations with Abyssinia, and their bearing on the political situation in the valley of the Nile, the Protectorate had become an Imperial rather than a purely Indian interest, and it is difficult to find solid reasons for a reversal of this decision. The argument that in case of military exigencies we must apply to India for the most speedy and convenient means of increasing the forces available on the spot applies equally to the other two East African Protectorates, to Ceylon, and other Eastern Colonies.

In any case the discussion would certainly be prolonged, and it would be a most unnecessary expense, and in other ways highly inconvenient that, in the meanwhile, a costly staff should be maintained at the Foreign Office for the sole purpose of supervising the administration of this small Protectorate, independently of those which in many respects are so closely assimilated to it.

Cab. 37/75/43

4 British Mandate for East Africa, 1919

... Whereas His Britannic Majesty has agreed to accept the mandate in respect of the said territory, and has undertaken to exercise it on behalf of the League of Nations in accordance with the following provisions ...

Article 3
The Mandatory shall be responsible for the peace, order and good government of the territory, and shall undertake to promote to the utmost the material and moral well-being and the social progress of its inhabitants. The Mandatory shall have full powers of legislation and administration.

Article 5
The Mandatory:
(1) Shall provide for the eventual emancipation of all slaves and for as speedy an elimination of domestic and other slavery as social conditions will allow;
(2) Shall suppress all forms of slave trade;
(3) Shall prohibit all forms of forced or compulsory labour, except for essential public works and services, and then only in return for adequate remuneration;
(4) Shall protect the natives from abuse and measures of fraud and force by the careful supervision of labour contracts and the recruiting of labour ...

Article 6
In the framing of laws relating to the holding or transfer of land, the Mandatory shall take into consideration native laws and customs, and shall respect the rights and safeguard the interests of the native population. ...

Article 10
The Mandatory shall be authorised to constitute the territory into a customs, fiscal and administrative union or federation with the adjacent territories under his own sovereignty or control, provided always that the measures adopted to that end do not infringe the provisions of this mandate.

P.P. 1923, vol. 24, Cmd 1794

5 Indians in Kenya

Colonial Office memorandum, 1923

1. General Statement of Policy

The general policy underlying any decision . . . must first be determined. It is a matter for satisfaction that, however irreconcilable the views of the European and Indian communities in Kenya on many points may be, there is one point on which both are agreed, namely, the importance of safeguarding the interests of the African natives. The African population of Kenya is estimated at more than 2½ millions; and according to the census of 1921, the total numbers of Europeans, Indians and Arabs in Kenya (including officials) were 9,651, 22,822 and 10,102 respectively.

Primarily, Kenya is an African territory, and His Majesty's Government think it necessary definitely to record their considered opinion that the interests of the African natives must be paramount, and that if, and when, those interests and the interests of the immigrant races should conflict, the former should prevail. Obviously the interests of the other communities, European, Indian or Arab, must severally be safeguarded. . . . But in the administration of Kenya His Majesty's Government regard themselves as exercising a trust on behalf of the African population, and they are unable to delegate or share this trust, the object of which may be defined as the protection and advancement of the native races. It is not necessary to attempt to elaborate this position; the lines of development are as yet in certain directions undetermined, and many difficult problems arise which require time for their solution. But there can be no room for doubt that it is the mission of Great Britain to work continuously for the training and education of the Africans towards a higher intellectual moral and economic level than that which they had reached when the Crown assumed the responsibility for the administration of this territory. At present special consideration is being given to economic development in the native reserves, and within the limits imposed by the finances of the Colony all that is possible for the advancement and development of the Africans, both inside and outside the native reserves, will be done.

His Majesty's Government desire also to record that in their opinion the annexation of the East Africa Protectorate, which, with the exception of the mainland dominions of the Sultan of Zanzibar, has thus become a Colony, known as Kenya Colony, in no way derogates from this fundamental conception of the duty of the Government to the native races. As in the Uganda Protectorate, so in the Kenya Colony, the principle of trusteeship for the natives, no less than in the mandated territory of Tanganyika, is unassailable. This paramount duty of trusteeship will continue, as in the past, to be carried out under the Secretary of State for the Colonies by the agents of the Imperial Government, and by them alone.

2. Future Constitutional Evolution

. . . It has been suggested that it might be possible for Kenya to advance in the near future on the lines of responsible self-government, subject to the reservation of native affairs. There are, however, in the opinion of His Majesty's Government, objections to the adoption in Kenya at this stage of such an arrangement, whether it take the form of removing all matters affecting Africans from consideration in the Council, or the appointment of the Governor as High Commissioner for Native Affairs, or provision for a special veto by the Crown on local legislation which touches native interests; and they are convinced that the existing system of government is in present circumstances best calculated to achieve the aims which they have in view, namely, the unfettered exercise of their trusteeship for the native races and the satisfaction of the legitimate aspirations of other communities resident in the Colony.

His Majesty's Government cannot but regard the grant of responsible self-government as out of the question within any period of time which need now to be taken into consideration. Nor, indeed, would they contemplate yet the possibility of substituting an unofficial majority in the Council for the Government official majority. . . .

Cmd 1922

6　Future policy with regard to Eastern Africa

Colonial Office Statement, 1927

. . . the administration of the East and Central African territories is based on the exercise by His Majesty's Government of a trust on behalf of the African population, and . . . while they may now be prepared to associate with themselves in that trust the members of the resident immigrant communities, they are still under an obligation to ensure that the principles of this trusteeship will be observed.

The responsibilities of His Majesty's Government for the territories of Eastern and Central Africa, with their 12½ millions of inhabitants, are of the very gravest character, and the possibilities of advantage to the Empire from the proper development of these areas are almost incalculable. . . .

It is therefore clear that before His Majesty's Government can formulate any final decisions upon these subjects a further Commission of Enquiry must be sent out to East and Central Africa. His Majesty's Government accordingly made the following announcement:—

His Majesty's Government consider, as a result of discussions between the Secretary of State for the Colonies and the Representatives of the territories in British Central and East Africa who attended the recent Colonial Conference, that some form of closer union between the territories of Central and Eastern Africa appears desirable, more particularly in regard to the development of transport and communications, customs tariffs and customs administration, scientific research and defence. They have therefore authorised the Secretary of State to send to Africa a special commission with the following terms of reference:

[Detailed terms of reference follow.]

. . . In making the declaration of policy involved in setting up a Commission with these terms of reference, His Majesty's Government wish to make it clear that they adhere to the underlying principles of the White Paper of 1923 entitled 'Indians in Kenya' (Cmd. 1922), both in regard to the political status and other rights of British Indians resident in East Africa, and also as regards the Imperial duty of safeguarding the interests and progress of the native population as trustees for their welfare until such time as they can take part more fully in their own Government and in the common affairs of all races inhabiting the territories. At the same time they wish to place on record their view that, while these responsibilities of trusteeship must for some considerable time rest mainly on the agents of the Imperial Government, they desire to associate more closely in this high and honourable task those who, as colonists or residents, have identified their interests with the prosperity of the country.

July, 1927   Cmd 2904

7 Native policy in East Africa

Colonial Office memorandum, 1930

One of the most important matters, if not the most important, dealt with in the Report of the Commission on Closer Union in the East African Dependencies (Cmd. 3234) is native policy and administration; and His Majesty's Government in the United Kingdom have thought it desirable to record formally, without further delay, their general policy towards the native inhabitants of East Africa and the principles to be followed by the East African Governments in carrying out that policy.

2. It is well at the outset to recall and quote the declaration of policy incorporated in the Kenya White Paper of July 1923 (Cmd. 1922): [The words on p. 177 are quoted.] . . .

3. With the statement in the White Paper of 1923 in all its aspects and with all its implications, as well as with the principle laid down in the Covenant of the League and in the Mandate for Tanganyika Territory, His Majesty's Government express their complete concurrence. They fully accept the principle that the relation of His Majesty's Government to the native populations in East Africa is one of trusteeship which cannot be devolved, and from which they cannot be relieved. The ultimate responsibility for the exercise of this trusteeship must accordingly rest with them alone.

It will be noted that this principle of trusteeship for the native population is in no way inconsistent with what has been described as the 'Dual Policy', if this is properly understood. The task and the duty of government in East Africa is, in fact, two-fold, though the division is not between administration for the immigrant races and for the native population respectively. On the one hand, it must be the aim of the administration of every territory with regard to all the inhabitants, irrespective of race or religion, to maintain order, to administer justice, to promote health and education, to provide means of communication and transport, and generally to promote the industrial and commercial development of the country. In all this range of work persons of every race and of every religion, coloured no less than white, have a right to equal treatment in accordance with their several needs. But in the East African communities, the duty of trusteeship for peoples 'not yet able to stand by themselves under the strenuous conditions of the modern world' involves, in respect of these peoples, not an alternative system of administration, contrasted with that adopted with regard to immigrant races who are able to stand by themselves, but merely an addition to, or rather a specialised application and extension of, the common administration of which the benefits are enjoyed by the whole population. It is with the additional benefits and the exceptional safeguards called for by the special needs of the peoples 'not yet able to stand by themselves under the strenuous conditions of the modern world' that the trusteeship for the native races is particularly concerned; and it is essentially to ensure the maintenance of these exceptional safeguards and the development of these additional benefits that His Majesty's Government must necessarily, as trustee, retain in their own hands the ultimate decision and the final control. . . .

. . . increasingly to associate the natives with Government through local native councils. A complement to this would be the co-option, from time to time, of exceptionally advanced natives on bodies such as Native Land Boards, and ultimately, wherever possible, their admission to full membership of such Boards. An essential part of this policy would be the reference to Native Councils for their consideration of all proposals seriously or particularly affecting native interests, and the communication to the natives, through whatever organs it may be practicable to use for this purpose, of full information regarding the plans and proposals of the local administration, and the laws which specially concern the native population. It will be the duty of the local Governments in this way to keep the native population as far as possible continuously informed, not only of the laws to which they will be subjected, but also of the principal developments of the administration. Moreover, His Majesty's Government consider that at least the way should be kept open to the possibility, at subsequent dates, of the separate administration of particular native areas, outside the limits of any considerable immigrant settlement, should this be deemed advisable.

On the social side, His Majesty's Government regard the objective to be achieved as a general improvement in the standard of native life, alike in economic conditions, in home circumstances and in the physical health of men, women and children, together with the spread of education in the widest sense. . . .

Turning now to the economic sphere, His Majesty's Government are of opinion that the main objective to be kept in view is the improvement of the general condition of the natives by encouraging them to make the most efficient use of their own resources for purposes of production, full regard being had to the principle that the native should be in fact effectively free to work, as he may wish, either in his own tribal area, or on his own individual holding of land, or (subject to proper statutory safeguards of the conditions of employment) in labour for wages outside the tribal area. . . .

Cmd 3573, 1930

G

8   British Government conclusions on closer union in East Africa

Government Statement, 1930

. . . His Majesty's Government propose to adopt the following scheme for Closer Union in East Africa:—

I. For the purpose of the social and economic development of the Colony and Protectorate of Kenya, the Protectorate of Uganda, and the Mandated Territory of Tanganyika, there shall be established a High Commissioner whose duties shall be of a two-fold character. [A detailed list of his duties follows.]

II. In respect of the duties specified in (B):—

(i) The High Commissioner shall be assisted by a Council, of which he shall be Chairman, consisting of three officers on the High Commissioner's Staff and twenty-one members, namely, seven for Kenya, seven for Uganda, and seven for Tanganyika.

(ii) The High Commissioner shall nominate all the Members of the Council . . .

. . . The suggested changes in the constitution of the Legislative Council of Kenya have been the subject of particular consideration by His Majesty's Government. The goal of constitutional evolution, in Kenya as elsewhere, is admittedly responsible government by a Ministry representing an electorate in which every section of the population finds an effective and adequate voice. But that goal cannot be reached at an early date in a community where it has so far been practicable to enfranchise less than one per cent of the population, and where the idea of any substantial extension of the franchise finds little general support. For the native African population, indeed, in so far as the tribal organisation is still the basis of its social organisation, the most promising line of development for the near future may well lie, not in any direct participation in the Legislative Council, but in the increasing importance to be given to the Native Councils—an importance to be manifested alike in a continuous widening of their functions, and in a constant communication to these Councils, through the District Commissioners or otherwise, of the various proceedings and proposals of the Executive Government, as well as the enactments or Bills of the Colony's Legislature.

8. The conclusion to which His Majesty's Government have come is, at this juncture, to leave the constitution of the Kenya Legislative Council substantially unchanged and to retain the official majority. . . .

Cmd 3574

XI

THE INDIAN OCEAN

British interests and the interests of the inhabitants
of British territories

Apart from extinction of the slave trade, British interests in the Indian Ocean were principally strategic and economic. While over-riding British control was still strictly maintained in Ceylon and Mauritius in the years covered by this book, the constitutions of both islands underwent change. Constitutional advance in Ceylon after 1910 was rapid. Experience in radical political association grew, and the most notable development in this field was the Ceylon National Congress founded in 1919. Allegiance to the doctrine of trusteeship for all sections of the population was explicit in the Donoughmore report on Ceylon of 1928.

1 Mauritius Charter, 1885

1 There shall be in and for the Colony of Mauritius a Council of Government constituted as herein after mentioned.

2 The Council shall consist of the Governor of eight ex-officio members of nine nominated members and of ten Elected members. ... The nominated members of whom one third at least shall be persons not holding any Office in the Public Service of the Colony shall be such persons not exceeding nine in number at any one time as We may from time to time appoint by any Instruction or Warrant under Our Sign Manual and Signet or as the Governor in pursuance of the powers hereby vested in him may from time to time provisionally appoint The elected members shall be persons to be Elected as herein-after provided. . . .

16 September 1885

P.R.O. C66/5112

2 The future of Zanzibar

(a) *Foreign Office correspondence, June 1890*

No. 1

The Marquis of Salisbury[1] to Colonel Euan-Smith[2]

(Secret.)

(Telegraphic.) *Foreign Office, June 12, 1890, 3 P.M.*

I am on the point of instructing you to propose to the Sultan (with the concurrence of Germany) that he should be under the protection and guarantee of Great Britain, through whom all his relations with foreign Powers should be conducted.

We shall probably propose to him later that he should cede to Germany, for an equitable money consideration, the strip of coast south of Umbe which he has farmed out to her.

Let me know if there is any other point on which you wish provision to be made.

No. 2

Colonel Euan-Smith to the Marquis of Salisbury.—(Received June 13.)

(Secret.)

(Telegraphic.) *Zanzibar, June 13, 1890*

Your Lordship's telegram, Secret, of yesterday.

In case of Sultan pressing the question, I solicit instructions as to whether guarantee of his Throne extends to successors. If so, might he choose his own successor, under necessary limitations, and subject to confirmation by Her Majesty's Government?

I presume no mention regarding purchase of German coast should be made until Protectorate is an accomplished fact.

No. 3

The Marquis of Salisbury to Colonel Euan-Smith.

(Secret.)

(Telegraphic.) *Foreign Office, June 13, 1890, 5.15 P.M.*

You had better now sound Sultan as to his acceptance of our proposed Protectorate. The guarantee would extend to his successors, whom he might choose himself, subject to concurrence of Her

[1] Secretary of State for Foreign Affairs. [2] Consul-General at Zanzibar.

Majesty's Government. I do not wish to mention purchase of German coast, if it is not necessary as a matter of good faith. It will be mentioned in Europe by the Germans if not by us.

Sultan had better keep his own counsel till the matter is declared here.

Cab. 37/28/40

(b) *Foreign Office memorandum, July 1910*
Zanzibar was taken under British protection by the Treaty between this country and the Sultan of 1890. This Treaty, however, was subject to the provisions of the Declaration of 1862, by which Great Britain and France engaged to respect the independence of the Sultan—a declaration to which Germany adhered in 1886. . . .

If and when the island dominions of the Sultan are handed over to the Colonial Office, some change will be required in the local administration. In view of the Declaration of 1862, the islands cannot be treated as a Colony or an ordinary Protectorate, and arrangements must be made for the continuance in some form of the Agency and Consulate-General and of the present Government of the Sultan, which consists of a First Minister, Financial and Legal Advisers, and various minor officials, who are practically all British subjects. There seems to be no reason why the Governor of the East Africa Protectorate should not eventually be the Agent and Consul-General for Zanzibar. . . .

July, 1910   Cab. 37/103/40

3   British naval control of East Africa

Admiralty memorandum, 26 February 1912
. . . So far as Great Britain is concerned, our strategic command of East Africa rests upon the complete chain of our possessions encircling that coast upon a circumference of which the centre is Mombasa; namely, Aden, the Seychelles, Mauritius, Durban, and the Cape. These bases should amply suffice for the watching of hostile ports on the coast and the protection of our India-bound commerce.

26.2.1912   W. S. C.[3]
                                                                Cab. 37/109/29

[3] First Lord of the Admiralty.

4 The Constitution of Ceylon, 1928

Report of the Special Commission

. . . Ceylon has come to an important and even critical stage in its history. The absence of social and industrial legislation is no doubt due largely to the important place which feudal ties, family help and private charity have always occupied in Ceylonese society. Modern development, by which Ceylon has been affected, has tended to make domestic and private charity unequal to the solution of the economic problems of these days and especially of those which beset cities like Colombo and Kandy. Although Ceylon has not become industrialised, and is never likely to be largely so, there is already evidence of gaps which have been left in the social structure by the absence of any poor law system, of workmen's compensation, of up-to-date factory legislation, of proper, or even decent housing for certain sections of people, of control over sweated trades or adequate facilities for primary education . . .

Another subject of vital importance is the promotion of agricultural prosperity and the well-being of the rural population. . . .

. . . The clash of the claims of rival races in the Colony alone furnish a series of administrative problems unknown in Great Britain. Every piece of preferment, every school grant, every subsidy towards research work raises this difficulty. . . .

The factors then which we have to consider in devising a new constitution are these: first that there are circumstances which make inadvisable the grant of full responsible government but that the time has come when a substantial measure of responsibility should be devolved on the elected representatives; that in the absence of a balance of parties the establishment of a purely parliamentary system of government on the existing British model is not suited to conditions in Ceylon; and that in view of the special nature of its problems, the compactness of its area and the nature of the training given by the existing constitution to the unofficial members, it would be inexpedient, if not impracticable, to insist on the exclusion from the purview of the Council of the executive business of the Government. . . .

The scheme which we have decided to recommend to His Majesty's Government . . . involves the constitution of a representative Chamber, to be called the State Council, which will perform dual functions and require dual organisation, legislative and executive. . . . Both the legislative and executive actions of the Council will require the assent of the Governor, who will be specially charged by Royal Instructions to refuse or reserve assent to measures which infringe certain clearly defined principles. But otherwise it will be seen that the elected representatives will be placed in a position to exercise complete control over the internal affairs of the Island. . . .

. . . In view of the backward character of social and industrial legislation in Ceylon, which has no provisions for relieving destitution, no workmen's compensation, only the most elementary of factory regulations, and no control over hours and wages in sweated industries, a good case could be made out for regarding the extension of the franchise as more urgent than any increase of responsible government. When a considerable increase in responsible government is being recommended, therefore, the question of the franchise becomes of first importance.

. . . we could not recommend a further grant of responsible government unless that government were to be made fully representative of the great body of the people.

. . . The present property, income and literacy qualifications for the franchise should be abolished and the franchise should be extended, subject to minor reservations, to all men over 21 years of age and to all women over 30 years of age who (a) apply to be registered as electors (b) have resided in the Island for a minimum period of five years. . . .

The qualification for membership of the State Council should be the same as that of the electors, except that no person should be eligible who has not a literacy qualification in English. . . .

1928
Cmd 3131

XII

THE PACIFIC OCEAN
Constitutional changes and stock-taking of controls and relationships

The main political development was Australian federation in 1901. Apart from that, the principal problems arose in connexion with sovereignty over territories south of the Equator and the functions and jurisdiction of the Western Pacific High Commission. North of the Equator, trade and naval defence were principal considerations in decisions on British jurisdiction or administration.

1 New Guinea

Colonial Office memorandum, 8 July 1885
When it was decided by the late Government to extend Her Majesty's protection and jurisdiction to a portion of New Guinea, it was anticipated that the Australian Colonies, at whose desire the Protectorate was established, would provide such funds as might be required for the administration, until the settlements acquired stability and the place become [sic] self-supporting.

It was intended that General Scratchley, who, as Special Commissioner, left England in November, 1884, should proceed to New Guinea without delay, and having established the beginnings of government, it was expected that he would be followed shortly by intending settlers from the Colonies, and that a more complete system of administration would be elaborated as the country became better known and the white population increased.

It was foreseen that, as Her Majesty has no legal authority over foreigners outside her Dominions, it would eventually be necessary that the Protectorate should be enlarged into Sovereignty, if it were found that settlement and trade showed a tendency to develop the country; and the Law Officers were accordingly consulted as to the legal measures that would be required.

Within a few days of the Law Officer's Report, and before General Scratchley arrived in Australia, on his way to assume his duties, the unexpected news was received of the German flag having been hoisted on a portion of the island; and it was at once apparent that the situation had changed materially.

The necessity of declaring British Sovereignty at an earlier date than had been contemplated had to be considered, and on January 24th the Colonial Governors were informed by telegraph that it was intended to declare as British Dominions everything included in the Protectorate. The Agent-General of New South Wales was at the same time told that the effectiveness of the administration will in a great measure depend upon the amount of contributions which the Colonies might desire to provide.

The Colony of New South Wales at once intimated that it was a misconception on the part of the Imperial Government to suppose that the cost of General Scratchley's establishment was to be borne exclusively by the Australian Colonies. Other Colonies took the same line, and they all protested against Germany being allowed to retain any portion of New Guinea. Such a protest was, of course, untenable, but on the 19th February Lord Derby telegraphed that Her Majesty's Government will not refuse to entertain the question of Imperial contribution, recognising that German occupation of part of New Guinea, contrary to the wishes of the Colonies, may increase obligations and difficulties; also that the duty incumbent on Her Majesty's Government of protecting native interests may reduce local revenue, and the decision to proclaim Sovereignty must increase the cost of establishment.

. . . Subsequent negotiations with the German Government have led to an agreement as to the division of the island of New Guinea, and the British Protectorate has been extended over various groups of smaller islands lying to the east and south-east of the large island of New Guinea. It is not proposed to proclaim British Sovereignty over the Protectorate until an understanding is arrived at respecting the funds to be contributed by the Colonies and the Mother Country respectively. . . .

JOHN BRAMSTON[1]
Cab. 37/15/41

Colonial Office,
July 8th, 1885

[1] Assistant Under-Secretary of State.

2 Hong Kong

Colonial Office memorandum, 19 December 1888

Colonial Military Contributions

Remarks on memorandum circulated to the Cabinet by the Chancellor of the Exchequer in reference to Hong Kong

. . . Certain stations are being fortified, not because there are Merchants and Planters established in them who have houses and possessions to protect, but because these several points have been selected purely from Imperial strategic considerations, and have therefore become increasingly open to bombardment. They are fortified on the one hand as secure bases for the operations of Her Majesty's Fleet, and as refuges in time of war for our Mercantile Marine, and on the other hand to prevent their becoming hostile bases in the hands of an enemy.

Taking, therefore, the case of Hong Kong . . . it has been defended, not because Messrs. Jardine, Matheson & Co., have embarked their capital in stores there, but because it is the nearest British port to the Russian, Spanish, and French possessions in the Pacific. From Hong Kong as a basis, the Russian ports of Vladivostock and Nicolaieff would be blockaded and perhaps captured in the event of war, thereby preventing the Russian cruisers from carrying on their depredations on the high seas, possibly as far as the Cape.

It is the increasing strength of Vladivostock and the large French forces now maintained in Tonquin and in Cochin China which have led to the demand for an increased garrison at Hong Kong, not the increasing riches of the colony as being likely to invite the cupidity of Foreign Powers.

If, therefore, the community of Hong Kong were non-existent, or incapable of contributing at all, it would still be necessary for this country to maintain a fortified naval base there, or abandon all hope of naval action in the China and North Pacific seas. It may almost be said that Hong Kong is being defended to give effect to the Imperial policy on the frontiers of Afghanistan, at Constantinople, and in Egypt.

. . . The principle sought to be laid down by the Chancellor of the Exchequer that the Imperial Government has 'a right . . . . to fix, in the last instance, the amount of the contribution,' is in fact a claim to enforce taxation without any form of representation; a principle which, after long experience, has been abandoned by this country.

Even in the case of a Crown Colony, it is not now possible to act in the high-handed manner which was practicable a quarter of a century ago, when the Duke of Newcastle was Secretary of State.

To force a measure on an unwilling Council in the teeth of the non-official members—putting aside, for the moment, the Government Officers, who would naturally hold views of their own on such a subject—would place a heavy strain upon our Crown Colony system.

What is now being done is practically a redistribution, to a partial extent, of the Forces of the Empire in conformity with the military requirements of the present day. In certain cases, this policy has involved the removal altogether of an Imperial garrison, *e.g.*, from Australia, New Zealand, and Canada. In other cases it has involved an increase: but this arises from strategical necessity, not from increased local need.

. . . according to the census of 1881—Hong Kong contained 160,000 people, and in 1887 the estimated population was under 186,000.

. . . of the above 186,000 over 175,000 are Chinese, many of them exceedingly poor, of whom 30,000 live in boats.

. . . Hong Kong is, and always has been, a free port. To this fact it owes its present prosperity in comparison with other ports. To intro-duce customs duties would destroy that prosperity and upset the whole course of British trade with the East. Such a proposal would be strenuously resisted by the whole mercantile and shipping interests of this country. . . .

Cab. 37/22/45

3 The Commonwealth of Australia

The Governor-General's Speech at the opening of the first Parliament, 10 May 1901

[The Governor-General] was pleased to deliver the following speech:
'GENTLEMEN OF THE SENATE AND GENTLEMEN OF THE HOUSE OF REPRESENTATIVES:

As the first Australian Parliament, you have been honoured with the presence of His Royal Highness the Duke of Cornwall and York as His Majesty's High Commissioner. . . .

The inauguration of the Commonwealth in January was conducted in Sydney with a splendour worthy of the spirit of union animating the citizens of every part of Australia. It is now that the people so joined ordain the initiation in Melbourne of legislation which, there is reason to trust, will go far to realize the high hopes of the founders of Union.

. . . You will be called on to deal with a number of legislative proposals of the highest importance. In the first place, it will be necessary to submit to you measures for setting in motion the machinery of the Constitution, and for adapting to their new condition the great departments, recently transferred, of Defence, Customs and Excise, and Posts and Telegraphs.

You will be asked to constitute a High Court of Australia, with an extensive Appellate and Federal Jurisdiction. It is hoped that the character of this court will be so eminent, and its powers so comprehensive, that its decisions will be accepted as final by the great majority of litigants.

A Bill will be introduced to create a commission for the execution and maintenance of the provisions of the Constitution relating to trade and commerce. It is intended to confer wide powers, judicial and administrative, on this body, so that in the exercise of its authority the interests of each State may be secured, consistently with those of the people of the Commonwealth as a whole.

A Bill to regulate the public service of the Federation will be submitted.

. . . Steps have already been taken to cope with the difficult matter of selecting the federal territory, within which the capital of the Commonwealth is to be built. . . .

Bills for the firm restriction of the immigration of Asiatics and for the diminution and gradual abolition of the introduction of labour from the South Sea Islands will be laid before you.

Measures are also in preparation to provide for conciliation and arbitration in cases of industrial disputes extending beyond the limits of any one State, for the placing of patents and inventions under one uniform administration throughout the Commonwealth, and for the grant of an uniform franchise in all federal elections by the adoption of adult suffrage.

Some time must elapse before the financial conditions of the Commonwealth will admit of provision being made for old-age pensions. It is, however, the desire of my Ministers to deal with the subject as soon as practicable.

As soon as the necessary data have been collected, Bills will be prepared relating to banking, and providing for uniformity in the laws regulating federal elections. Navigation, shipping, and quarantine are among the subjects of proposed legislation, and consideration is being given to the best means of taking over, converting, renewing, or consolidating the public debts of States.

. . . The fiscal proposals of any Federal Government must be largely dependent on the financial exigencies of the States. The adoption of the existing tariff of any one of these States is impracticable, and would be unjust. To secure a reasonably sufficient return of surplus revenue to each State, so as fairly to observe the intention of the Constitution, while avoiding the unnecessary destruction of sources of employment, is a work which prohibits a rigid adherence to fiscal theories.

Revenue must, of course, be the first consideration; but existing tariffs have, in all the States, given rise to industries many of which are so substantial that my advisers consider that any policy tending to destroy them is inadmissible. A tariff which gives fair consideration to these factors must necessarily operate protectively as well as for the production of revenue.

The relations of the Commonwealth with the Islands of the Pacific have been occupying the earnest attention of Ministers, who have taken such steps as seem to them prudent for the protection of Australian interests in this regard, without in any sense embarrassing the international relations of His Majesty's Government.

The question of the construction of a railway connecting with these eastern communities the vast and hitherto isolated State of Western Australia has been under consideration. Examinations of the country intervening between the railway systems of South and Western Australia are now in progress, together with other inquiries. It is hoped that they may result in showing that the undertaking is justifiable.

Isolation was the chief obstacle to the early adoption of the Constitution by Western Australia, until the hope of closer connexion influenced the people of the West to risk the threatened perils of that political union of the continent which their vote at the referendum did much to complete.

. . . As soon as practicable after the necessary Act has been passed, means will be taken for the judicious strengthening of the defence of the Commonwealth. . . .

. . . Intercolonial free-trade will be established in the very act of imposing a Federal Tariff. . . .

Parliamentary Debates, Commonwealth of Australia, 1901

4 Fiji Letters Patent, 21 March 1904

. . . 8. From and after the coming into operation of these Our Letters

Patent the present Legislative Council in the Colony shall cease to exist and there shall be in and for the Colony a Legislative Council constituted as hereinafter mentioned.

9. The Legislative Council shall consist of the Governor as President, ten official Members, six Elected Members and two Native Members. . . .

C 66/5203

5 Weihaiwei

Colonial Office memorandum, 7 June 1904

Weihaiwei, which is roughly 1,300 miles from Hong Kong, 90 from Port Arthur, and 40 from the Treaty port of Chefoo, consists of an island and a strip of the mainland—over and above the sphere of influence behind the latter. The leased territory, including the island, has an area of 285 square miles, with a population of 150,000; the sphere of influence has an area of 1,500 square miles. The island, unlike the mainland strip, is the private property of the British Government. It was bought by the Admiralty and War Office. Naval views as to the value of Weihaiwei seem to vary from time to time, but the main difference of opinion is as to whether the place should be fortified or not. There is apparently no doubt as to the excellence of the harbour. . . .

7 June, 1904   C. P. L. (Lucas)[2]
Cab. 37/80/166

6 Bill to amend the 1872 Pacific Islanders' Protection Act

Colonial Office memorandum, 12 June 1906

The Pacific Islanders' Act, 1872, was passed in consequence of the outrages and irregularities committed in connection with the recruiting of labour for Queensland, and, to a less extent, for Fiji.

. . . Since 1872 circumstances in the Pacific have entirely altered. Recruiting for Queensland has altogether ceased, owing to the passing of the Commonwealth Pacific Islanders' Act, 1901. Fiji has become a British Colony, under the direct control of the Secretary of State; and the recruiting of Pacific Islanders for service there is very small, coolie

[2] Assistant Under-Secretary of State, Colonial Office.

immigration from India having taken its place. The Gilbert and Ellice Islands have now been for more than ten years under a settled administration as a Protectorate; the Solomon Islands are also administered as a Protectorate, and are expected to develop rapidly; and in the New Hebrides there are both British and French Resident Commissioners, who, with the co-operation of the Naval Officers and of the numerous missionaries, are in a position to supervise European settlers.

It may be added that in the last-named group an elaborate system of government, including detailed regulations for the recruiting and service of native labourers, will be set up if the proposals embodied in the draft Anglo-French Convention are ultimately accepted.

The remainder of the Pacific Islands are all subject to settled administrations. The only group that is not now definitely under the control of a European Power is the New Hebrides. In these circumstances it is submitted that the drastic provisions of the Pacific Islanders' Protection Act, 1872, are no longer necessary. . . .

12 June, 1906   Cab. 37/83/55

New Zealand refused to join the federation of the Australian colonies. There are extracts from the Report of the Royal Commission on Federation, 1901, in *Speeches and Documents on New Zealand History* edited by W. D. McIntyre and W. J. Gardner (1971). There are also extracts from a debate in the New Zealand parliament in 1927 on the Singapore naval base.

READING LIST

Mansergh, P. N. S.: *The Commonwealth Experience* (London, 1969).

Duncan Hall, H.: *Commonwealth: A History of the British Commonwealth of Nations* (London, 1971).

McIntyre, W. D.: *Colonies into Commonwealth*, 2nd edition (London, 1968).

Cambridge History of the British Empire, Volume III: *The Empire-Commonwealth* (Cambridge, 1959).

Bennett, G. (ed.): *The Concept of Empire: Burke to Attlee, 1774–1947* (London, 1962).

Wight, M.: *The Development of the Legislative Council, 1606–1945* (London, 1946).

Oliver, R. A. and Fage, J. D.: *A Short History of Africa* (Harmondsworth, 1970).

Oliver, R. A. and Mathew, G. (ed.): *A History of East Africa*, Volume I (London, 1968).

Harlow, V. and Chilver, E. M. (ed.): *A History of East Africa*, Volume II (London, 1965).

Wilson, M. and Thompson, L. M. (ed.): *The Oxford History of South Africa* (London, 1969–71).

Fage, J. D.: *An Introduction to the History of West Africa*, 4th edition (London, 1969).

Wrong, H.: *Government of the West Indies* (Oxford, 1923).

Toussaint, A.: *History of the Indian Ocean* (London, 1966).

Spear, T. G. P.: *The Oxford History of Modern India, 1740–1947* (London, 1965).

Morrell, W. P.: *Britain in the Pacific Islands* (London, 1960).